How to Have a
H.E.A.R.T.
for Your Kids

Rachael Carman

RESOURCES FOR THE HEART AND MIND

How to Have a H.E.A.R.T. for Your Kids

Published by Apologia Press

A division of Apologia Educational Ministries, Inc.

1106 Meridian Plaza, Suite 220/340

Anderson, Indiana 46016

www.apologia.com

Manufactured in the USA

First Printing: February 2011

ISBN: 978-1-935495-41-3

Cover design: Doug Powell and Anderson Carman

Book design: Doug Powell

Printed by Courier, Inc., Westford, MA

Unless otherwise indicated, Scripture quotations are from: *The Holy Bible,* New International Version © 1973, 1984 by International Bible Society, used by permission of Zondervan Publishing House.

This book is dedicated first to my kids: Charles, Anderson, Savannah Anne, Molly, Elizabeth, Joseph, and Benjamin. You fill my heart with joy each day! I am so grateful that God pursued, healed, and opened my heart to love and grace. You are each growing up to be such wonderful people. May your hearts be filled with God's love, and may you desire His will and His way above all else! I also dedicate this book to all the moms who have lost their hearts somewhere out in the world. My prayer is that in some way this little book will bring you closer to your children.

Contents

Introduction
The Heart of the Matter

Several years ago I was asked to share with a homeschooling group about the "heart issue" of homeschooling. I was not given an outline, but a topic: "How to Have a Heart for Your Kids." I thought and prayed about it, and as I prepared for the presentation at our state conference, I took the word "heart" and turned it into an acronym:

H — Have a heart for the things of God
E — Enrich your marriage
A — Accept your kids
R — Release them to God
T — Teach them the truth

I peppered the presentation with plenty of examples from my own homeschooling journey, also known as

Mr. Toad's Wild Ride. This teaching seemed to resonate with my audience, as many moms told me they had been affirmed and encouraged.

Then I was asked to consider turning the presentation into a book. I struggled with this idea because writing is so different from speaking. So many of the audiences I had spoken to knew my family's story, and this particular presentation made sense to moms who had the benefit of this foreknowledge. But unless my readers were already familiar with our family, well, the notion of a book seemed like a birthday cake without a party: What's the point? So I hope you'll indulge me as I provide a little background.

Having told our story over and over to audiences all over this great country, I am amazed at how it touches so many lives and hearts. Yet I can take no credit—God wrote it that way, not me! It is my prayer that our story will bless you and that it will bring you closer to the Master and help you point your children to Him as worthy and able.

Has Anyone Seen My Heart?

The short version of how we got into homeschooling is simple: There was a lot of yelling and screaming. In fact, I was ready to quit almost before we started. Our party line to family and friends was, "This is just for kindergarten. Surely we can't mess that up!" Our plan at that time was to just get through the one year. Mere survival was the goal.

True confession: I had lived most of my life principally concerned about myself, and all in all, I had been rather successful. I had my faith all mapped out from a young age: I went to church, sang the songs, recited the verses, and knew the facts. What I lacked was a real, growing, intimate relationship with God. After I married Davis, we continued to go to church, but I still did not need God; He was only fire insurance.

Then God blessed us with a son. I remember thinking when I held him at the hospital, "Are they really going to let me take him home? I don't know how to do this! What if I mess it up?" Now, you must understand that there were many friends and family who would, and some eventually did, help me with the new challenges I was facing. Yet I did not want to admit to needing help from anyone.

Eighteen months later, Charles discovered (as every child will at some point) that he was independent of me and that he could exert himself and his will. Indeed, he was by-the-book strong-willed. Charles knew at a young age what he wanted, and he had an amazing determination to get it. In fact, he was one of those kids that was willing to die on every hill!

During this time, we had a great pediatrician, Dr. Elberson, and a great friend, Paulette Gates. They supported us in our goal of positively redirecting Charles's strength of will. They encouraged me to keep up the fight, assuring me that it would all be worth it in the end.

Living for Someday

I looked forward to the start of school almost before Charles was born. I had taught public high school in Texas and performed some homebound instruction in Ohio. I loved teaching! I loved the classroom, and I loved the challenge. But I also knew that I wanted to be home for my kids. I knew that was important. But the fall of 1990, when Charles was a newborn, when the leaves were changing and the buses started their routes, I was already dreaming of returning to my passion.

I think it should be noted here that we were planning on having only one child, maybe two. (This marked a notable increase from the "no kids" napkin agreement we had once signed together in a restaurant. But that's a story for another time.) As I sat on the front porch of our seventy-year-old home on Paxton Avenue in Akron, Ohio, full-term with my firstborn, watching the students making their way into the high school across the street, I dreamed of the day I would go back to teaching full-time.

God is so good to go before us, leading us to places we never intended to be, much less wanted to go. On this particular street there lived five stay-at-home moms. One of them, Courtney Fairfax, had been praying that God would send other moms to the neighborhood, and He answered her prayers. We were still settling in when new neighbors, the DiPaulos, moved into the home on the adjacent corner. Davis went over to meet them, and when he got back, he mentioned a word I had never heard before and which would significantly change our lives, though not for five more years. That word was "homeschooling."

Lesa DiPaulo was planning on homeschooling her two young daughters. My first question was "Why?" Once I got to know her, she seemed smarter than that. What was she thinking? She was gracious and patiently explained that she thought it was best for their family and that it would encourage the growth of their family relationships. I listened, not at all interested—not even amused.

Now that I was a new mom, I set about meeting the other moms in the neighborhood, and I learned there were two others who were homeschooling. Was it something in the water?

I thought the choice to homeschool meant these moms had nothing better to do, that they had no passion, no dream, no drive. I figured they just couldn't let go of their kids and get on with their lives. Or perhaps the parents simply couldn't afford to send the children anywhere else. I feared their poor kids would become socially inept outcasts, unable to work with others or solve conflicts.

They proved me wrong in living color.

God is so good. I was privileged to watch these young women and their families live out loud in front of me for three years that proved foundational in our preparation for homeschooling. For the three years Courtney, Kathy, Lesa, Carolyn and I were neighbors, we had a regular Bible study together, we gardened together, and we watched each other's kids. We laughed and cried, shared life together, and grew close. I came to know these women as lovers of their husbands, children, and their God. They were faithful, seeking to obey and honor their heavenly Father in all things. They were not the weirdos I had made them out to be. No, these were women of God willing to sacrifice themselves to be all He had planned them to be. God was real to them. He was part of their every decision.

And their kids? Their children were the most polite I had ever known. Conflicts were resolved in a timely manner, apologies made, and relationships strengthened. It was just about an ideal neighborhood situation.

This was the experience of a lifetime, and it became a reference point for my life, a safe time and a time of great blessing that I often return to in my mind.

Moving On

Then came the time to move away from Akron. The office where Davis was working was about to go under, and though he was not out of a job, it was time to look. I admit it: I was ready to move back to the South. This Texas girl was ready to defrost. Snow in April and May and chilly fireworks on the Fourth of July were not my cup of tea. Davis had tried to warn me about the winters; he had wanted to stay in the South all along. Now I was more than ready to get back to the heat and humidity. And so it was that Davis took a job with the same company that would move us to Charlotte, North Carolina.

I was thrilled. I could already feel the sun on my skin.

Yet moving was bittersweet. I had been so blessed by the women in my neighborhood. Even though I was hopeful for the future, I knew in my heart that we had all been a part of something I might never get to experience again. We had a party in the park, they gave us a picture collage, and we said good-bye. At the time, I underestimated the long-term impact these friends would have on my life.

In choosing a new home, our highest priority was the schools. Charles would soon be nearing school age, and the public schools in Charlotte were undergoing a transitional growth period marked by changing school assignments, teacher shortages, and bond issues. Keep in mind that homeschooling was still nowhere on my radar screen. I had a plan, and it included a big yellow school bus.

Our initial move to Charlotte proved to be more than a little complicated. The following details are of no real relevance to our homeschooling journey, other than to leave no holes in the story. We found a house and moved straight in upon arrival in May. We were there long enough to paint, wallpaper, put up a fence, and get connected at a church. Essentially, we were in town long enough to exhale. Then the company moved us back to Akron in the spring of 1994.

We moved back unhappily and were there for twelve months when the company changed course once more and moved us back to Charlotte in June 1995. Shortly after our arrival in town, Davis began looking for a new job and started with a new company in May 1996, just after the birth of our third child and first daughter, Savannah Anne.

Praying for His Teacher

With this second move to Charlotte, we again focused on schools. It was now time for Charles to start kindergarten. We could not afford a private education, so we purchased a house in the "best school district" in town. I had it all planned out: This was the year I got my life back. This was the year that Charles would go to school and Anderson (our second boy) would go to preschool two days a week. I would have time alone with little Savannah Anne. I had visions of joining a Bible study again, cleaning house and having it stay clean, completing some long-neglected projects, and having lunch with friends. This was going to work out perfectly.

After we enrolled Charles, we were asked by the school to submit a letter as to what we wanted in a teacher for our child. They wanted to know our child's strengths and weaknesses and our desires and dreams for his educational experience. Wow. We hadn't expected this. Davis wrote a detailed letter, and we began to pray for Charles's teacher. In July, we were invited to an open house and met his new teacher. In retrospect, there were many glaring red flags, most of which we were blind to. Nevertheless, we were underwhelmed. When we got to the car, Davis turned to me and asked, "Is that the teacher you have been praying for? Because that is not who I have been praying for." I felt the same way.

So we continued to pray for his teacher, and I kept planning my life. We had it all worked out. Davis would take Charles and the neighbor boy to school in the morning on his way to work, then the neighbor mom would meet the boys at the bus stop and walk them home. It was perfect. Charles was off to school, and I didn't have to leave the house. Everything seemed to be going off without a hitch.

The Yellow School Bus

On the first day the kids were suppose to wear a tag with their bus number pinned to their clothes. Charles was tagged with #809. He was all smiles, off on a new adventure. But that first day he did not ride to school alone. We all loaded up the car and took him to school as a family, complete with pictures. Interestingly, the teacher seemed even less like what we had prayed for, but what could we do?

That afternoon, as I went out to check the mail and meet my son after his first day of kindergarten, I saw my neighbor come over the hill with her dog and her son, but mine was missing. "He wasn't on the bus," she told me.

I ran into the house and called the school. The secretary responded, "That must be who this is sitting here."

I called Davis, and he left work to pick up our son and bring him home. On day two, Davis took the boys to school and went inside to talk to the teacher and get the plan straight. We even retagged Charles so that there could be no mistake—he was to return home on bus #809.

So that afternoon I went down to check the mail and meet my son after his second day of kindergarten. Again I saw the silhouette of my neighbor, her dog, and her son, but mine was nowhere to be seen. I didn't wait for an explanation—I went to the phone.

"He's not here," I was told. "He was put on the wrong bus."

Davis was hot. Again he left work to retrieve our son. Charles seemed more upset this time. Davis talked with the secretary and the principal and found out that the teacher was the one responsible for getting the kids on the right bus. He then made the point that she had failed to do this two consecutive days despite the tag, which still clung to Charles's shirt.

Though the principal was sympathetic, he was unwilling to change Charles's teacher per Davis's request. He asked us to please just forgive her and go forward and let this thing work itself out.

Work itself out?! What if Charles had gotten off of the bus just because he was ready to stop riding around aimlessly? What if someone had picked him up? What if . . . ?

We decided to keep Charles in school as we moved on up the chain of command to secure a change in instructors. In the meantime though, Charles was unwilling to ride the bus. By now it had completely lost its appeal. My plan was quickly unraveling as I joined other parents in the afterschool pickup line, all because his teacher couldn't read a tag.

But that wasn't all. The neighbor boy was bringing home papers, and Charles wasn't. I mean, nothing. This seemed strange to me, because when he was in preschool I practically needed a suitcase to lug everything home that he did each day. Charles had been in kindergarten for twelve days, and the only thing he had brought home was a "How I did today" slip.

Davis had made several phone calls, but no change in teachers was forthcoming. The principal controlled teacher assignments, and he was refusing to budge. Finally, on day thirteen, Davis took the day off from work to visit Charles's class. Davis went to school with Charles at 7:30 a.m. and was home with him by 12:30. He described it this way: "It wasn't like anything bad was going on. It was more like nothing was going on. Just filler, nothing impressive. Nothing."

So Davis took the radical step of withdrawing our son from public school.

Now What?

I had been afraid of this possibility. While Davis was at school that day with Charles, I had investigated every available option to salvage my plan and my life. I had called every one of the too-expensive private schools in the area. I made appointments and put us on waiting lists. I had formulated Plan B.

When Davis came home that afternoon, I don't even remember asking how it went. Instead, I immediately launched into my proposed option. We had appointments to keep, a plan to enact—no time to waste!

We were off in a hurry, running all over town with promises of admission in anywhere from a couple of days to a few weeks. This was great. It was going to work out after all. Or was it? When we finally got home with three exhausted kids, I was all out of words but convinced we had a feasible plan.

Davis finally spoke. He mentioned the obvious issue of finances. How were we going to pay for this? It wasn't in the budget. And how long were we going to do this? Just this year or for the long haul?

Then he asked the question: "What about home-schooling?"

Davis says that my head spun on my shoulders and I responded in my most unattractive and selfish voice. I said, "Oh, yeah, great. Let me get this straight: You get to go to work, and I get stuck here all day with the kiddos. This was the year I was supposed to get my life back!"

"I was just thinking," he continued patiently and gently, "we have been praying for months for Charles's teacher, and I think we have been praying for you."

The words were like a hammer against my hard heart, a shock to my dead senses, a long-overdue wake-up call. The Holy Spirit had spoken through my husband, piercing straight through to my heart. I was speechless.

Okay, But Just for This Year

Let me be clear. When we made the initial decision to homeschool, it was to be a short-term fix. After all, I couldn't mess up kindergarten, right? Being the planner that I am, and being convicted by my husband's words, I was now faced with formulating Plan C. I knew enough to understand that I really didn't know what I was doing. I needed to make some calls.

My first call was to a local homeschool mom I barely knew. She gave me two pieces of advice that I still give to others as they start: First, she said, I needed to relax. She said that homeschooling is more than an educational choice—it's a lifestyle. (At that moment in my life I couldn't appreciate the depth of that bit of wisdom.) Then she said something that stunned me: "Relax and read to your kids. Get to know them—their strengths, their weaknesses, their interests. Then you will know where to go with curriculum, but you don't need any now."

Get to know them? What did she mean? I knew my kids. Didn't I?

Then I phoned my friends from Paxton Avenue back in Akron. Talk about eating humble pie. (It's not too tasty, by the way.) I got in touch with Carolyn first, and I think that she just about collapsed. Was I serious? After all, I had made fun of her, to her face, for homeschooling. Carolyn just laughed, though it had to have really blessed her. She promised to pray for me, and I received my first glimpse of what God had done for me in advance by giving me those friends back in our old neighborhood up north.

The First Year

Confession time again: When we started homeschooling in the fall of 1996, I did not have a heart for my children. Although I loved my children, I was ready to get my life back. I was done with the motherhood gig, ready to get back to me.

I learned that year that in many ways I did not know who my kids were, though it would be accurate to say I knew who I wanted them to be. I had a plan for them to make me look good, but I had not considered what God's plan might be for their lives. I knew what they liked to eat—what kind of pizza they preferred and their favorite snacks. I could pick out their favorite clothes. I knew their favorite cereal, ice cream, and cartoons. But what else had I taken the time to learn? Not much.

I didn't see my children as a trust or a blessing or a gift. Not really. Perhaps in words, but not in deed, not in my heart. No, in all honesty, I thought they were slowing me down, keeping me from what I really wanted to do, and often I saw them as an inconvenience. Of course, I would have never said this out loud. I would have vehemently denied the implication had anyone suggested it. But in my heart—my hard, crusty heart—there was only me. All of the "sacrifices" I had made had been for show, not from the heart.

Our first foray into homeschooling was rough. Oh, I threw myself into it, but I found myself mourning the death of my expectations. Everything had changed. Charles and I had not been together 24/7 in three years, since he first entered preschool. As I've mentioned, he was strong-willed—a character quality he had inherited from me. I understood how he operated but had little patience for it. I was certain he was the answer to my mother's prayers. You know the one: "I hope you have a child like you someday!" Okay, my mom is not really like that, but I remember calling and apologizing profusely on more than one occasion after Charles had given me a fit, realizing that I must have done the same to her.

I wish I could say that I unerringly heeded the

wisdom I had gleaned from my friends. I did not. I began by ordering a reading program. I went to the local teacher supply store and purchased charts and writing pads. I even bought a lesson plan book. After all, I had the training to do this. I had been a teacher.

My first priority was getting Charles to read. It was slow going. It would have been nice had someone told me then that he would be a late reader albeit an avid one. Our days were often punctuated with tears as I tried to conform him to my perfect plan. I expected him to make me look good by reading, and he simply wasn't cooperating.

Still, Charles and I were having a good time. We were laughing together more, and I discovered that I liked him. That December, Davis remarked that he thought we were actually growing closer instead of becoming more contentious. Was this possible?

The Heart of the Issue

In the spring of 1997, several homeschooling pioneers were encouraging us to attend the annual state homeschooling conference in Winston-Salem. Davis and I saw this as an opportunity to get away together for a few days. Our plan was to go so that we could say we did, but we had no intention of getting in any deeper. We secured childcare for the kids and headed to the conference.

By the time we checked into our hotel room, I had developed a slight fever and was not feeling well. Nevertheless, we headed out to register for the conference and take in a workshop. We had been advised to spend our time upstairs, being encouraged in the workshops and seminars, not downstairs in the book fair with its myriad curriculum choices. That shouldn't be hard, we thought. We weren't there to shop. We had no intention of homeschooling for the long haul.

We literally wandered into a workshop hosted by Chris Davis of the Elijah Company. Remember, we just wanted to be able to say we went—we really didn't care which seminar we attended. Yet during the next hour our perspective, attitudes, and subsequently, our lives were changed. By the end of the workshop we were both in tears, convicted by the Holy Spirit as to His call on our lives. It was awesome.

Needless to say, we attended several workshops

over the next couple of days. There was energy and inspiration everywhere we looked. There were thousands of parents, some of whom had brought their children with them. They were parents just like us—normal, seeking, discovering new possibilities.

No one in the curriculum hall was selling a replacement heart. Besides, I hadn't known that mine was missing. But now I knew it would be a key component in going forward on this new adventure. And I was anxious to move forward, but I would need to recover my heart first.

But how?

I am so grateful to be able to tell you that the seemingly impossible is possible. You can recover your heart. It may be lost, but it can be found. Your heart might be wounded, but it can be healed. It may even be broken, but it can be mended. The Great Physician is waiting and more than willing to help you in this process—and He makes house calls!

Just like the Tin Man in *The Wizard of Oz*, I got a brand-new heart. I am more vulnerable, more open, but I'm also more invested, more joyful, more contented, and more full than I ever thought possible. I had bought into the world's lie that I had to harden my heart to find happiness as a modern woman, when in fact, true joy can come only by keeping the heart tender. I had been taught to guard my heart, to remain suspicious of others who might seek to destroy it or ridicule it. However, it turned out that the key to happiness was to entrust my heart to Him who alone is able to keep it until the day of His coming. As a result of trusting Him with my heart, I have come to know the peace that passes understanding. This book is a compilation of lessons I learned along the way to this revelation and in the days since.

I'm guessing that some of what I just shared is familiar to you. Maybe you too have found yourself at an intersection of life where you never expected to be standing. Perhaps you also made light of homeschooling because you couldn't understand the "why" of it. Maybe you've felt the call to homeschool but ignored it and pushed it down, hoping it would go away. Maybe you knew it would mean certain sacrifices that you never really wanted to make.

Or maybe you're experiencing emptiness in your

relationships with your children. You have given them everything—toys, trips, trivia, teams—but you've given them no target, no testimony, no Teacher. You may have met the legal requirements and cultural standards for educating your kids but have yet to give them your heart.

Do you want to reclaim your God-assigned place in raising your kids? Do you want them to have a heart for others and for the Lord? Do you want to build a growing relationship with them that will transcend every challenge you might face as a family? Do you want to get started today? Are you ready to navigate new terrain and take some practical steps toward heart recovery? Yes? Then let's get started!

Chapter 1
H: Have a Heart for the Things of God

*"You will seek me and find me when you
seek me with all your heart."*
Jeremiah 29:13

*"But seek first His kingdom and His righteousness,
and all these things will be added to you."*
Matthew 6:33, NASB

This may seem like a strange place to start, but it really
is the only place to start. In order to reach the hearts of
your kids, you must first have a heart for the things of
God. If you want to direct your kids on a course of seeking and desiring God above all else, if you want them to
worship Him alone, if you want them to obey His call on
their lives, then you must set a clear example of seeking,
desiring, worshiping, and obeying Him. It starts with
the parents. You cannot pass on what you do not have.
In order to develop a heart for your children, you must

develop a heart for the things of God—His word, His truth, His grace, His people, and His church.

"Intentional parenting" means that we are thoughtful and purposeful in our actions and words. As intentional parents we do not react, but we respond. We do not panic; we pray. We do not give sermons; we give scripture. And we are prepared to do so through our own pursuit of God, for His glory and by His grace. By seeking God first, we are going before our families, paving the way for our kids. We are clearing a path through the undergrowth that is everyday life and showing our children how to put Him first in all things.

All things have a starting point—a place where it all began, before which there was nothing, only emptiness. "In the beginning God," the Bible says in Genesis 1:1. This first verse of the Holy Scriptures lays the foundation for the rest of the story. The Word begins by acknowledging the moment when God first spoke creation into being, a time before which there was nothing. This is the same place we must start as we set out to have a heart for our children. We must begin with God.

Having a heart for God means that we put Him first,

that we pursue Him and honor Him and model these
things for our kids every day.

Whose Character?

When we first started homeschooling, I really thought it
was all about educating my kids. No, that wasn't it. Not
at all.

I thought it was about choosing the right curriculum.
Hardly.

I thought it was about following a well-planned scope
and sequence. Uh-uh.

Then I began to think it was all about shaping my
children's character. (They did need some work.) But I
got over that quickly.

In fact, it was *my* character that needed the most
work. After all, my kids were watching me and, well, let's
just say, "Monkey see, monkey do." As I came to recognize the true nature of the work God had set before me,
the course He had designed to "conform me into the image of His Son" (Romans 8:29) and sanctify me for His
divine purpose, then I *began*. My beginning point was to
realize just how much I needed Him.

There was only one problem: I didn't really know Him. And since I didn't know Him, I doubted He knew me or noticed me or, truthfully, even cared. After all, I was just an ordinary person, no one special. Surely there were more important people in whom God needed to invest His time. And so I didn't really think He would do anything miraculous in me. Miracles were something He didn't do anymore, right? All that business of parting the Red Sea—that was Old Testament stuff, not for the twenty-first century. There were no Jericho walls to come a-tumbling down in modern-day North Carolina. He just didn't do that sort of thing anymore. And I was okay with that. I was not the needy type anyway. I was pretty sure I had it all under control.

Daily Living (a.k.a. Discipleship)

Our children are constantly watching us whether we want them to or not. They are seeing it all. And they don't just watch—they imitate. I have both laughed and cried when I've seen how keenly my kids observe my behavior. When I see how meticulously they butter and cut their banana bread into four strips per slice—just like me—I laugh. But when they speak to one another curtly and impatiently, I am ashamed to have been their example and in some way responsible for their attitudes.

We are admonished in Scripture to be imitators of Christ (Ephesians 5:1). God's plan is that we would watch and learn from Him. Through worship, study, and prayer we are to walk with Him and, consequently, become more and more like Him. In the meantime, our kids are to be witnesses of our transformation and start imitating Him through imitating us. See how beautiful His plan is for the discipleship of our kids?

That's what Deuteronomy 6:6–7 is talking about when it says of God's commands, "Impress them upon your children, talk about them when you sit at home and when you walk along the road, when you lie down and when you get up." The writer is describing in simple language what discipleship means, how it looks, and when it happens. This is the model of what it means to walk with God. The discipleship of our kids is an ongoing process and should permeate every aspect of our daily lives. We should not just talk about our dependence upon God in tough times or in desperate times, but every day and at all times.

God's Power Revealed in Nature

So who is this God? If having a heart for your kids has to start with having a heart for the things of God, what do you do if you don't even know who He is? The good news is that you can start to come to know Him as soon as you decide to. To me one of the most amazing things about God (and there are too many to list) is that not only did He make each of us individually and uniquely, but He desires to have a relationship with each of us individually and uniquely. In Psalm 139 the writer says that God knit you together in your mother's womb, that God saw you in the secret place and wove you together, that your very days were numbered by Him before you were even born. Luke 12:7 says that even the hairs on your head are numbered. Now *that* is individual and unique.

Okay, so God knows you. Where do *you* begin to know *Him?* Well, there are a couple of places. In Romans 1:20 and Psalm 19:1–4, we are told that all creation points to the Creator. In other words, when you look at the world and the wonders of nature, you are looking at the handiwork of God. The intricacies of a lily, the majesty of a mountain, the power of a waterfall, the delicate wings of a butterfly, the precision of a spider's web, the beauty of a sunset—these not only demonstrate but accentuate the hand of the Master. By observing, studying, and admiring the work of His hands, we are able to get a glimpse of God's own nature.

Have you ever been simply overwhelmed by a beautiful landscape? Ever marveled as you watched a robin builds its nest? Ever considered the design of a hummingbird? a whale? a bumblebee? Have you ever tried to count the stars or find a rainbow's end or hide from a storm? Have you ever been walking in the woods and found yourself caught up in the wonder of it all—the majestic trees, the living moss, the water rolling over the rocks, the breeze among the leaves. Or maybe you were at a zoo with your kids when you stopped to consider the creativity of God—the blue feet of the booby, the rhino's horn, the zebra's stripes, the elephant's trunk, the camel's humps, the monkey's tail. Who thought of all of those things, those amazingly unique things? Only God.

It was He who gave the mountain goat the ability to survive on jagged peaks, the bat the ability to fly in the dark of night, the paper wasp the skills to build its home, and the eagle wings to soar. It was He who made the rose, the sunflower, the redwood, and the magnolia. He paints the sunrise and the sunset, gives texture to the beach and dimension to the mountains. The Bible says that He knows when a sparrow falls (Matthew 10:29) and He clothes the lilies of the field (Matthew 6:28–29). He made it, He knows it, He takes care of it. All creation worships Him and points to Him. "Through him all things were made; without him nothing was made that has been made" (John 1:3).

Metamorphosis

Nature offers so many analogies and metaphors. One of my favorites is the metamorphosis of a caterpillar into a butterfly. These two things don't even *look* similar. Our family has raised caterpillars. The first time was when we stumbled upon some swallowtail butterfly eggs on a patch of parsley in the back yard. My daughters were picking some just for fun when they noticed the tiny orange spheres on the underside of the plants and brought them inside. Anderson, our resident animal expert, researched the discovery and announced that we would soon have caterpillars on our hands. I admit, I doubted his conclusion. They seemed too small to really be anything. But Anderson was right. Just a few days later we had about twenty tiny black caterpillars covering the parsley and gorging themselves on it.

The little creatures started out about as long as the width of your pinky fingernail and no thicker than a thread. But in no time at all they were the size of my entire index finger. As they grew they molted, and eventually they had bright yellow, green, and white stripes. I couldn't believe the amount of parsley these creatures ate. We would give them a fresh supply in the morning, and by the evening they had reduced it to mere stems.

We kept our caterpillar collection in the kitchen and would often set it in the center of the table at mealtime to watch them eat. Sometimes, if we were really quiet, we could hear them munch. Try it sometime. There is no real way to describe the experience.

Finally, after about two weeks, the caterpillars prepared for their ultimate "molt." They crawled to the underside of a stick and made themselves a sling to sort of lean back into. Then they attached themselves to the stick and became very still. A couple of times we missed this step by just a few hours and found only the green chrysalis upon our return. As a result of these near misses, we resolved to watch the entire process, no matter how long it took. We didn't want to miss the construction of the oblong green capsule.

Of course, we weren't able to see the transformation taking place inside the chrysalis. We knew there were dramatic changes going on in there, but from the outside they were undetectable. In fact, if you didn't know something was happening, if you didn't know to anticipate the change, you wouldn't have guessed you should.

So every day we waited and marked the days off our calendar in anticipation of the new creature's emergence. The first one started showing signs of emerging on a Sunday morning during breakfast. The chrysalis began to wriggle around like something was trying to break out, but unfortunately we missed the actual egress as it happened while we were gone to church. When we returned, there it was: a brand-new creature. Here was a completely new insect, not at all like the one we had fed parsley to.

Nothing was the same—not its size, not its colors, not its features, not its eyes, not its diet. Nothing.

Metamorphosis. Total and complete change.

We watched as the new butterfly flapped it wings and straightened them out. We put fresh flowers in its cage now, not parsley, so that the new creature could feast on nectar. We sprayed the flowers with water so that it could drink. We kept the butterfly for a couple of days. Then, after a long discussion, we came to the conclusion that it needed to be free, it needed to fly. The caterpillar had only needed to eat—it didn't care where or in what space. It only craved the parsley. It didn't appreciate the outdoors, and neither did it seem to need sunlight. But the butterfly was different—it needed to be free to soar. Somehow it seemed to long for the sun on its wings and the breeze in the air. And of course it was drawn to the flowers. So we all went out on the porch and opened the cage and let it go. It was hard to watch, but it was also exciting to keep an eye on our former charge until it flew out of sight.

We were worms once, those of us who are saved. Now, having put on Christ, we too are new creatures.

"The old has gone, the new has come!" (2 Corinthians 5:17). If we have put our hope and trust in Christ Jesus as our Lord and Savior, then all things have been made new. Through His creation, God has given us a very clear picture of the transforming power of the blood of His Son. We start off as worms, interested only in ourselves, only with what is directly put in front of us, with no real aspiration, no hope, no freedom. But we have the hope of salvation through the process of justification—our acceptance of Christ's sacrifice on the cross in our stead. When we choose His death and, in fact, die to ourselves, He does what only He can do. He changes us as we submit to Him, His will, and His way in our lives. As we do this, we make ourselves vulnerable, just like the caterpillar does as it sits very still waiting for the change to take place. Then it happens: the unexplainable. Our hearts become radically different. We look different, we talk different, we eat different, we walk different, and ultimately, we fly—we fly home to be with Him upon His glorious return!

God's Heart Revealed in His Word

God did not place us on this earth without instructions, rules, or purpose. He placed us here for one primary reason: to bring glory to His name. And He tells us how to do this in His Word. Sounds easy, doesn't it? But it isn't. If glorifying God were so clear-cut and obvious, then we ought to be able to do it all the time. So why don't we? We don't because at our core we are a selfish, fallen, and sinful people. Yikes! What a lethal combination! In fact, without Christ, we are doomed, trapped in ourselves with no way to bridge the gap between our sinful state and our need for redemption.

But God . . .

I'm not sure there's a more powerful word pairing in the English language.

But God . . .

This phrase is used throughout the Bible to signify a turning point—from peril to rescue, from chaos to control, from fall to redemption. We were once lost in our sins, "But God, being rich in mercy, because of His great love with which He loved us, even when we were dead in our transgressions, made us alive together with Christ (by grace you have been saved), and raised us up with Him, and seated us with Him in the heavenly places in Christ Jesus" (Ephesians 2:4–6, NASB).

Truly amazing. We choose against Him, willfully and deliberately. Yet He has made a way for us to return across the chasm created by our sin, and that way is His only Son, Jesus Christ.

You see, the Bible is the greatest love story ever told. It's the story of a Father and His love for His children—a faithful, sacrificial, unconditional love.

> *Amazing grace! How sweet the sound*
> *that saved a wretch like me!*
> *I once was lost, but now am found.*
> *Was blind, but now I see.*

As we read and study the Bible, the story of God's love for us all—and for each of us individually—we come to know Him through its pages, its stories, and its precepts. We read of our Father's provision for His people in the wilderness. We read of His justice when

Adam and Eve disobeyed His only rule. We read of His patience with Jonah, His faithfulness with Abraham, His defense of Job, His love for David, and His kindness toward Ruth. We read of the strength He gave to Samson, the courage He gave to Joshua, and the perseverance He gave to Nehemiah. We read the prayers of Hannah as she longed for a son, Mary as she rejoiced at being the chosen mother of the Christ, Hezekiah as he asks God for help. We read David's songs of repentance, comfort, and praise.

Through each of these true stories, we come to know our Father as a real, living Sovereign who is active in the daily lives of men. The men and women who appear in these pages are emotion-filled, problem-riddled, soul-needy flesh and blood. Gideon, Noah, Miriam, Esther, and Nehemiah are all people like you and me, people we can relate to and learn from. They needed God and called out to Him. He answered them, blessed them, and never left their side. Thus a study of God's Word gives hope to even the most weary, discouraged, overwhelmed, and lost among us.

Through daily study of the Bible, God gains dimension in our hearts and imaginations. We come to know

Him as a living God, the one and only true God. His word shows Him to be infinitely patient, wise, loving, and forgiving. As we learn more and more about this God, we are drawn into a relationship with Him, even as our eyes are opened to His holiness and our sinfulness. We are confronted by His provision in His one and only Son as the answer to our lost condition.

The Old Testament tells us of His Law and the impossibility of keeping it. It's here we learn the price of sin, which is death. But the Old Testament also tells of a hope in the coming Messiah: "And he will be called Wonderful Counselor, Mighty God, Everlasting Father, Prince of Peace" (Isaiah 9:6).

The New Testament begins with an account of the complete fulfillment of the Old Testament prophecies and God's divine answer to our desperate need for redemption. The four Gospels tell of Jesus' birth, His life, His death, and His resurrection. We learn of His time on the earth with family and friends, the disciples He chose, the miracles He performed, and His teachings. Here we meet Peter, John, Mary, the woman caught in adultery, and the woman at the well. We see Jesus feed a multitude with nothing but a few fish and loaves of bread. We witness Him sleeping in a boat and teaching in the temple. We see others fall before Him in worship, desperate, thankful, and often broken.

We read of Jesus' march toward Jerusalem, His jaw set, knowing what is to come. We witness His last night with His friends as He washes their feet and they share a meal, their last together. We are told they even sing together. Then comes the betrayal, the one He anticipated but dreaded. The one that was necessary but still painful. The one that surprised the other disciples but couldn't surprise Him. Gethsemane and the prayer, the soldiers, the arrest, the trial, the cock's crow, the whipping, the mob's cry for His crucifixion, the cross bearer, the nails, the centurion, Mary and John. Then, "It is finished" (John 19:30). Darkness falls over the land and the earth quakes. His side is pierced, and He is laid in a borrowed grave with a hurried burial before the onset of the Sabbath.

Early that Sunday morning—there has never been a more anticipated sunrise in all of history than that one— all the heavenly host held its collective breath then jointly exhaled as the devil was defeated. The payment for sin was made once for all and for all time. And with the resurrection of the Son of God, our hope was established. We were thereby granted the opportunity to live with Him in heaven forever, free from sin at last. Now *that* is some good news!

The remainder of the New Testament chronicles the early days of His church. In letters inspired by God and written in the hand of His chosen apostles, we receive not only direction on how to live by faith, but also encouragement for enduring difficult trials. These letters thoroughly cover the call to holiness and what it means to be set apart for God. Several of the letters are written to various new churches, admonishing and encouraging them to live lives worthy of that to which they have been called—to flee from sin, to suit up for battle, to stand firm, and to not be surprised when they come under attack. These same letters give you and me strength to fight the good fight and perspective to visualize and finish the race as we face many of the same challenges encountered by Christians so long ago.

If we seek God in His Word, we will find Him, when

we seek Him with all of our hearts. This is just one of the many promises given by our promise-keeping God. Not only does He offer us a better life—He delivers. Through the study of His Word, our faith will grow and our hearts will find hope, healing, and forgiveness.

God's Grace Revealed Through Prayer

I started out on my homeschool journey thinking I had everything under control. I had a schoolroom set up, charts and graphs, pads of paper, and fat pencils. I even acquired a real chalkboard! (I've always loved them.) I set to work all by my confident self. Sure, I called a few friends who freely and graciously gave me advice—good advice which I promptly ignored, thinking I knew better, bless their hearts. After all, I was a trained professional educator, and I should know how to do this. Right? Wrong. I had been trained to teach a roomful of strangers, not individuals and not my own children. I had been trained to teach the mind, not to reach the heart. My training had not prepared me for this.

One day it happened: a challenging day in which my measure of patience was not enough. Not nearly enough.

I white-knuckled my way through it, but I was fooling no one, least of all the kids. I needed help. Not professional help, but the providential kind. I needed God. He had been waiting for me to come to a place I now call Way Out Beyond Myself. This is the place where I am in way over my head, well beyond my own abilities to accomplish anything without Him. It's not a pleasant place—not at first anyway—but now . . . well, let's just say I have made it home. How can I say that?

Simply put, I like it out here in Way Out Beyond Myself because it's where I get to see my God show off the most. It's much harder to see His glory under the city lights when distractions are flashing all around me. Out here there are no artificial lights to hide the stars, and His glory shines brighter. Out here my back is to the "sea," much like the Israelites when the Egyptian army was bearing down on them. Out here I know I have no way of escape, no plan B, and frankly, no apparent hope. Out here is where He shows up and shows off, and it's an awe-inspiring spectacle.

For me, having a heart for the things of God began with me calling out to Him in desperation. I was in dire need of His help. I had finally realized that I didn't know *what* I was doing, much less *how* to do it. Another co-op or a different curriculum wasn't the answer—He was. I had been raised my whole life in church, and I remembered the stories of His coming to His people's rescue, so I prayed and hoped He would hear me, too. And He did.

When I asked for wisdom and direction, He gave them freely. He even started to show me things I hadn't asked for, things I hadn't realized I needed. He went before me, just as His Word says He does, and He made a way for me in the wilderness.

I started praying each week *before* I prepared and planned for the week of school. I saw that when I laid out the plans before the Lord, as Hezekiah did in 2 Kings 19:14, that He would lead me beside still waters. He would show the way. When I forget about this important part of my planning time, frustration quickly sets in during the week and I become overwhelmed and distracted by stuff that will not matter in the long run. But when I come before the throne of grace on my knees, in humility and submission to His will for our home school, then He remains my focus. It is through these times of prayerful seeking that He shows me "great and unsearchable things" I do not know" (Jeremiah 33:3). And there is so much I do not know.

Jesus in the garden is my example for this. The scene is sobering to consider. Can you imagine your son begging you to find another way, anything but the one you have set before him? Can you picture your daughter begging to the point of sweating blood yet ending her appeal by saying, "I trust you, and I will do what you think is best"? That's the point where I would give in—at the point of utter submission, when I know I have my child's heart, is when I would say, "Okay, let's do this another way." After all, God did this for Abraham when he lifted his knife to sacrifice his son (Genesis 22:1–13).

But that's not what happened when Jesus prayed in the garden. No, when it was God's one and only Son, He didn't stop the nails, even though Jesus was completely submissive. There was no other way. This had been the plan from the beginning, and it had to be carried out for the ultimate benefit of all mankind.

God wants our total humility and submission. It is a beautiful sight for Him to behold when one of His children kneels at the foot of His throne, seeking Him. I believe that it honors Him for us to take this approach to His purpose and plan for our lives and the lives of our children.

Don't you love to hear from your kids? Isn't it tremendous to hear the longings of their hearts? I don't mean their "wish" list; I mean their heart's desires—what they value and hope for. As my children get older, these are the conversations I enjoy most. I love to hear how they are growing spiritually, where they are feeling challenged, what they are considering, what books they are reading. As they share, I can sometimes see or sense something they are oblivious to or something they have misinterpreted. When we talk, I can see where their hearts are and how to help them achieve God's best for their lives. How much more then can our heavenly Father do the same for us when we talk with Him?

The Bible also says we are to pray continually (1 Thessalonians 5:17). I don't know about you, but I always have plenty to pray about. I wake up in the morning asking for wisdom to handle what lies ahead. I wake the kids, asking God to bless their day. At breakfast we thank

Him for His gracious provision. Then someone is rude to someone or grabs or yells or something, and I pray because I am in danger of slipping back into my old habit of sermonizing. At a time like this, God wants me to seek Him, ask Him for insight, and wait for Him to touch my child's heart.

God's Glory Revealed When We Worship Him

Now that you're getting to know Him, now that you're reading His story and about His love for you personally, are you feeling like you just might burst with awe and wonder? He has provided an outlet for that, too. It's called worship. This is where we acknowledge Him for who He is, and acknowledge who we are not. And that's cause for a celebration!

It's been said that God is most glorified when man is enjoying Him most fully. I know of no way to enjoy God more than to worship and praise Him. When you realize who He truly is, you will not be able to hesitate. You will not be able to worry, you will not be able to panic. You will simply throw up your hands and praise Him. And you should. We all should. We have been given so much, and He has been so good to each of us. No matter our circumstances, the provision for us to be reconciled to Him (i.e., mercy) and the gift of salvation (i.e., grace) are reason enough to praise Him.

Our praise should be complete, total, unashamed, and enthusiastic. After all, we were made for worship. We were made for this! Think about it. Without our propensity for worship there would be no Hollywood, no NFL or NBA, no *People* mmagazine, no *American Idol*. There would be no fan clubs or popularity contests or marketing departments. No, if we weren't wired by God to be awed, we wouldn't yell for our team, we wouldn't wave flags, and we wouldn't argue about who is the best at everything under the sun.

True, our emotions can sneak up on us. We get excited about a happy ending and sad about a tragic one. A beautiful scene can overwhelm us with delight, while a depressing scene can overwhelm us with despair. One look at our finances or to-do list and we can find ourselves on the proverbial rollercoaster in the dark, going up and down and around the bend unpredictably. But that's not how God intends for it to be. Though we have been given emotions, it is His desire that we keep them in check and rule over them instead of allowing them to rule over us.

Worshiping God alone is the key. Too many times this is the part we neglect, the part we leave out, the part we are uncomfortable with. We seem perfectly content at a sporting event to raise our hands, sing and dance, and proclaim our love for the home team at the top of our lungs. Some of us are even willing to do those things when worshiping God in a private setting but feel uncomfortable doing so at church or even in front of our families.

Do you want to have a heart for your children? Then first have a heart for God. And don't be afraid to show it. Get your hands up. Praise Him out loud. Pray and lift Him up. Memorize His Word all you want, but without the heart change, without true worship, it's empty.

HEART CHECKUP

1. Having a heart for God requires self-discipline. Do you have a regular quiet time? When? Where? Is it a priority for you? Do you have a plan for studying God's Word?

2. How would you characterize your prayer time? Do you spend time praising God and thanking Him (Psalm 71:8; 92:1). Do you confess your sins (1 John 1:9) and make your requests known to Him (James 4:2)?

3. What are some things you need to praise God for regarding your children? What should you thank Him for? Ask forgiveness for? Ask His wisdom and guidance on?

Chapter 2

E: Enrich Your Marriage

"For this reason a man will leave his father and mother and be united to his wife, and the two will become one flesh." This is a profound mystery—but I am talking about Christ and the church. However, each one of you also must love his wife as he loves himself, and the wife must respect her husband."
Ephesians 5:33

"Rise up, my love, my fair one, and come away!"
Song of Solomon 2:13

The E in our HEART acrostic stands for "Enrich your marriage," though it didn't start out with this meaning. I had been giving this presentation for years when God changed my outline. Davis and the kids were accompanying me to an event in the Raleigh area. The trip had been a series of bumps—car trouble, a couple of sick kids, miscommunication with the hotel—and now we were arriving late. We had booked two rooms because we were bringing the whole family—nine of us in all. I made the mistake of assuming those two rooms would be adjoining, as our oldest was not yet a teenager. Unfortunately, we were given two rooms separated by a floor. That just wasn't going to work.

So we had to convince the manager of a sold-out hotel that we were fine with the three girls in one bed, three boys on the floor in sleeping bags, and one in a porta-crib. I'm sure we were violating a fire code, but what were we to do? Besides, the kids were excited. Sleeping all together in one room, and on the floor to boot, sounded like a grand adventure to them. I, on the other hand, was in need of an attitude adjustment. I'd had grand ideas of the kids enjoying the Discovery Channel in the next room as I relaxed and reviewed with my notes in the other. Instead, I was juggling the nine of us through a single bathroom and puzzling out sleeping arrangements. I had forgotten my reading light, and when it became necessary to turn off the lights so that the baby could get to sleep, I lay there tossing and turning and praying that God would help me with my presentation.

As usual, on the morning of an event, God woke me early. One of the kids was snoring as I threw on some sweats and made my way down to the lobby to squeeze in some quiet time and study. I was down there for about an hour when Davis called to say that the event coordinator was planning on picking me up in an hour. An hour?! Davis said he would get the kids up and take them to breakfast, so I could have the room to get ready to go.

The rush was on. I had barely gone through my outline once and now I was hauling myself back up the stairs praying out loud that God would put it all together, that I would greet the kids with grace and enthusiasm, and that He would bless them through this ministry He had called me to.

Not surprisingly, I arrived to a room of chaos.

There were simply too many people and too little space. Everyone was hungry, and most were still sleepy. Davis cycled everyone through the bathroom while I nursed a baby, changed a diaper, and brushed tangled hair—all at once. Finally, the kids were dressed and ready. The sudden silence in the room took my breath away, then panic set in. I had exactly twenty-five minutes to work a miracle.

I rushed through my shower, rehearsing my outline and going over specific points by memory. I kept getting hung up at E. Then it happened: God spoke to my heart. *Rachael, we need to change that one. You can put those insights under A. You need to make your E stand for "Enrich your marriage."*

I stood there in the shower, having not completely rinsed off, as a timer ticked loudly in my head reminding me that time was refusing to stand still. "What? No. I can't do that today. I hear you God, but not today. I don't have time to do that right now. I wasn't ready with what I've *already* researched. Please don't make me change it now. I can do it next time, okay?"

But the idea nagged at me as I dried off and started doing my makeup and hair. God poured out so much that I had to stop several times to jot down all He was showing, reminding, and teaching me. Somehow the twenty-five minutes stretched out, and I had plenty of time to complete the arduous process of making myself presentable.

I headed downstairs both excited and anxious. I was excited because I knew He had given me a specific point for the specific audience that day. And I was anxious because I had not researched or prepared for this particular point.

My hostess and I had a nice visit on the drive to her church, where she introduced me to the team of women who had put the event together. She then showed me to a room where I could make final preparations. God was so good. I really needed this quiet time, and I didn't even have to ask!

When I had finished my presentation, God was faithful to affirm His change to my outline with stories from several attendees. Many told me what a difference it had made in their lives to watch their parents love on each other and how it had given them security. Others cried as they confessed to having neglected their marriage relationship, now realizing that it had been detrimental to their children's lives. Several went home that day resolved to make changes by the power of the Holy Spirit and to honor God by being better wives to their husbands.

I have since become convinced that this point is indeed pivotal to developing a heart for our children. We must strive to consciously and intentionally enrich our marriages. We must be investing in the relationship with our spouses. Our children desperately need us to do this.

Our communities, our churches, and our country needs us to. And God commands us to. He wants to show Himself to the world through our marriage relationship. There are so many lessons and insights that can be wonderfully demonstrated in the context of marriage—selflessness, sacrifice, and service, just to name a few. And of course, there is the picture of oneness that is represented so beautifully by the intimacy of marriage.

Living a Defense of Marriage

How many of us have signed petitions in support of defining marriage as a union between one man and one woman? How many have been appalled at the advances made by proponents of same-sex marriage? How many have spoken out against it? How many voted against it? Now for the tough question: How many of us are living out a marriage that is worth defending?

Have you ever thought about it in this way? Have you ever thought about what you are living "out loud" in your marriage? Do you live like you actually love your spouse, or even *like* him? Do you live like you are glad you said, "I do"? Have you ever thought about the fact that people are watching and learning from your marriage, including your kids, your friends, your neighbors, and even strangers?

The mantra of the homosexual community is that if two people love each other they should be allowed to marry. They claim it is a natural expression of their love for one another. What about us? As heterosexuals, are we willing to fight as hard in our marriages to keep the love alive, or are we more willing to let it go, to give up, not realizing the trust we have been given? What about our marriages is worth defending? Our sacrifice for one another? Our commitment to each other? Our covenant before God? Our kids?

It's easy to add our signatures to a list, cast a vote, or hold a sign. It's much harder to discipline ourselves, to determine to defy our flesh, to die to ourselves, to consider others before ourselves. Too often we are willing to do the easy thing and hope it's enough. We prefer that it not require any real change on our parts, either personally, in our homes, or in our hearts. But if our daily lives do not exemplify sacrifice, service, love, and forgiveness, then we nullify our votes and negate our signatures. In essence, we lose—not because we are defeated, but because we don't fight. We give up, lie down, and refuse to engage. If our marriages don't measure up to the standard we say we support, then we will have failed.

However, failure is not inevitable. Victory is ours for the taking. How? We must change one marriage at a time, one heart at a time, one home at a time. Talk about a grassroots movement! We need to stop criticizing others and begin looking inward and clean up ourselves. We have some corners to dust, some floors to sweep, some sticky spots to attend to. And in some cases, the cleaning is the least of our worries. There are walls to move, attics to empty, and rooms to repaint! Think of it as a marriage makeover, one that gives rise to a brand-new heart to operate with—a whole heart, healed and ready to love.

Whatever

Wait a minute. Isn't this book about how to have a heart for your kids? So why all the talk of marriage? It is from watching their parents' marriages that our children learn trust, sacrifice, loyalty, teamwork, forgiveness, cooperation, communication, and responsibility. It is from our marriages that they learn perseverance, joy, diligence, kindness, gentleness, and communication. It is from our marriages that they learn grace.

Isn't that what it is all about, learning how to walk in grace? Imagine what the world would be like if we all walked in grace. You see, the world has substituted tolerance for grace. This is a cheap exchange if ever there was one. Tolerance means I forego biblical love and its standards. It means I let you do whatever you want to do, as long as it makes you happy, and you let me do whatever I want, as long as it makes me happy. With grace, holiness is the highest objective; with tolerance, happiness becomes the objective.

Scripture calls us to holiness. We are to encourage one another, spur one another, sharpen one another, and admonish, rebuke, and instruct one another toward that goal. Conversely, tolerance says, "Hey, whatever makes you happy. Don't bother with God's law if it makes you uncomfortable. No, whatever you think is best, you go for it." Tolerance says it doesn't matter who God is or what He thinks. Yikes! We need to sound a warning here. We're talking about God, and it *does* matter. It matters profoundly and eternally.

He is holy, and He calls us to holiness. Obedience is often uncomfortable, but in this place we are promised love, joy, peace, patience, kindness, goodness, faithfulness, gentleness and self-control as listed (Galatians 5:22). If we make tolerance paramount in our marriages—as in "You do your thing and I'll do my thing, and we'll split everything fifty-fifty if it doesn't work out"—then we teach our kids to give in to their own selfish desires apart from God. We teach them that the most important thing in life is to find themselves and pursue their dreams, ignoring anyone who gets in the way. Tolerance does not raise the bar; it actually eliminates it.

Such an approach to marriage does our children a great disservice. They are depending on us to direct them in paths of righteousness, to point them to something and someone outside of themselves, toward a purpose that has eternal consequences and rewards. We need to point our kids toward the values of sacrifice and selflessness as seen on the cross of Calvary. This is the standard of ultimate love defined by dying to oneself and living for the Lord. Now *that* is something worth living for.

So often I hear parents say that what they want most for their children is for them to be happy. We can either give our kids the world's empty notion of happiness, which will lead them down any number of dead-end paths in pursuit of an evasive feeling, or we can point them toward the real joy found only in following Christ's example of selflessness. This path is not a dead end. It is narrow, but it is the path that leads to life.

No One Told Me

I remember being in the hospital after the birth of my first child. The delivery had been difficult. Perhaps the doctor should have sent me home to wait out the final two weeks of my pregnancy, but instead he chose to induce labor. I didn't know any better. Before it was over, they had to use a suction cup to pull my son out as a resident literally pushed on my abdomen with both hands. It was like being unable to wake from a bad dream.

Then they handed my baby to me.

Behold the handiwork of God! Talk about "take your breath away." Here was this little seven-pound person we had been waiting for, yelling and screaming and covered with goo. I had no idea then the impact he would have on my life.

You know, when you're young, no one tells you how hard life is going to be, much less marriage. Would we listen if they did? It seems to me that self-sacrifice is something best learned under duress, when we're least expecting it. After all, no one in their right mind would sign up for it. We're much more likely to rush to sign up for situations we think are all about us, and we ignore the seemingly obvious sacrifices that will need to be made. And so we've refashioned marriage to be self-serving, not self-sacrificing. In fact, we have made individualized marriages an art form in this culture. So many young people have removed from their ceremonies thoughts and words about growing together as one. Rather, the focus has shifted to the "beauty" of two people supporting each other in their individual pursuits, not the coming together of a man and a woman as one flesh (Genesis 2:24).

What if we started living out God's original intent for marriage—oneness? What if we were willing and excited about sacrificing ourselves for our marriage? What if we sought God first and honored Him in our marriages by seeking to serve our spouses with our words and actions? What if we lived marriages worth defending, worth emulating, worth desiring? What if our marriages pointed others to God and His power to work in the lives of broken, humble, normal men and women who want to glorify Him in all things? What if?

The world needs an answer, a standard, a hope, a security that our marriages can represent. Of course, Jesus is the answer. His grace and forgiveness played out in our marriages paints a beautiful picture of His perfection in our weakness. It's what the world needs now. Oh, that we would surrender to His healing work and sanctification. This constant striving to make it on our own, to prove we can do it without God, that we don't need Him—well, it would be funny if it weren't so sad. He is our only hope. Telling the world about that hope starts in our homes and in our marriages.

Take a Stroll

So how do you keep the spark in your marriage? Or how do you put the spark back? At the risk of oversimplifying the issue, I say have fun again! Why not start with a stroll down memory lane? Remember when your love was young? Remember when you went on dates, when you held hands, your first kiss? Remember those long conversations on the phone late at night? Do you recall his laugh, his touch, the newness of it all? What about the proposal? Setting the date, the rings, telling friends, picking out an apartment. Remember when it didn't matter how you spent your day, as long as you were together? Remember planning the wedding, the dress, the flowers, and the cake? Remember all the energy you had back then, the adrenaline rush, the high of young love, the kissing? Do you remember the kissing? Can you think back before the diapers, midnight feedings, ear infections, and bedtime tantrums? Remember when the two of you carried on complete conversations, before the untimely knocks on your bedroom door?

Think for a moment. What do you wish you could recapture? What do you seem to have lost? What would you be willing to do to get it back? Would it mean you have to let go of some hurts? Would it mean forgiving yourself for mistakes you've made? Might it require you to embrace grace, acknowledge your desperate need for

Christ, and extend that same grace to your spouse?

As great as young love is, I wouldn't trade it for what Davis and I share now. The rush and newness of it all was wonderful, but the years and shared experiences are far better. Yet when I think back, there are so many great memories. I get a chill when I consider what it will be like for my own children to find their future spouses.

Davis and I met in June and were married that same December. The only way I can explain the whirlwind nature of this courtship is that my mother had wisely encouraged me to pray for my husband and I had done so for several years. When I met Davis, I simply recognized him as the one I had been praying for. It was as though I had known him for years, and the feeling was mutual. I wouldn't say we were unusually mature for our age, but God did what only He can do and went before us, then confirmed His will for us.

Our life together has been one wild ride; there's nothing normal or average about it. But I would guess your story is similar. We all have amazing stories and adventures that God has carried us through. Here's a brief look at some of ours:

- ♥ Davis put me through the last two years of college.
- ♥ We had a foster child for eighteen months.
- ♥ We moved across the country when I was pregnant with our first child, toting a dog and three antique cars (Davis's hobby at the time).
- ♥ We've lived with in-laws.
- ♥ We survived a house fire.
- ♥ We were called to homeschool when we had three children. Now we have seven.
- ♥ In a fifteen-month period, we sold a house, built a new one while living in a small rental, welcomed the arrival of our seventh child, wrote a book, and moved into the new house.
- ♥ Not long ago, during a two-year period, we experienced unemployment, a church split, a business purchase, a new church home, a growing ministry, and our oldest son's graduation.

This list is not exhaustive, just a few highlights.

What about you and your spouse? What curves has life thrown you? Where has your adventure taken the two of you? Green pastures? Beside still waters? Through the valley of the shadow of death? Take a moment to map it out. Now go back and acknowledge God in those places. You know He was there, don't you? His Word says that He never leaves or forsakes us (Deuteronomy 31:6). Oh, it might have seemed dark or lonely or confusing, but He was always there and always will be. Life gets hard because we are living in a fallen world, but He is with us and He comforts us—if we let Him.

When I recount God's faithfulness during our journey, I am overwhelmed by His patience and grace. He has been so good to me especially. I can see now, in retrospect, when He held me, carried me, cried with me, intervened for me, and performed miracles on my behalf. Davis and I have grown so much as a couple. Yes, we had opportunities to quit and give up. There were intersections where it would have been easier, at least momentarily, to take an exit ramp and check out. Only by God's grace and strength have we come this far.

We have worked at our marriage, both of us. We are

not passive partners but active allies, guarding well what we have been given. We have chosen to value each other, to spend time together, to respect, to listen, to grow, to challenge, and to encourage one another. We have not given into the crises of middle age but, rather, are exhilarated by our future together.

A Note to Wives

Ladies, our men, our husbands, they need us. They need us to respect them, to follow them, to trust them, to admire them, to love them, to want them, to support them. The world would have us treat our men (given to us by the Creator of the universe) as incapable, irritating dolts. I know too many women who have fallen prey to this attitude. Oh, it starts innocently enough—just a little giggle, the rolling of the eyes, or an unspoken grumble—but don't think they don't notice.

I do not watch much television anymore, but I used to. One of the reasons I watch less these days is because I came to realize Hollywood's sense of humor is not very funny. Typically, our TV programs make fun of male of the species, especially traditional-minded men who open doors for women and believe in purity. Generally, men are depicted as empty-headed slobs who lack self-control, chase women, and indulge in all manner of foolish behavior. Men are still pretty universally thought of as jerks if they leave their wife and kids, and yet they're often portrayed on television as has having been stupid for getting married in the first place.

At the movies, men occasionally come off better. Leading men are often depicted as romantic, sensitive, and thoughtful. Then there are the movies in which men play warriors or protectors who conquer distant lands and brave new worlds. These kinds of films are watched mainly by men because they can appreciate the characters. These male moviegoers dream about living courageous lives, fighting for what's right, and saving the day. Women don't seem to get this. They often dismiss these movies as being too violent to offer any redeeming value. I'm not saying that many warrior-type movies are not over the top in terms of violence; they are. But the point is that men dream of having something they love enough to fight for and being able to defeat anyone or anything that might threaten that loved one. They long for us to support that need by cheering them on in whatever they do for a living or even as a hobby.

The last few decades have been difficult for males, especially the conservative or traditional ones. Some-where along the way it became acceptable for husbands and fathers to be made fun of in the media. Some may ask, "Who cares?" We all need to care, because this kind of humor comes at a price that is quite expensive. In stereotyping traditional male roles as silly and inconse-quential, we lower the bar. Our expectations plummet, and a self-fulfilling prophecy is soon realized. We have only ourselves to blame when men start to behave like irresponsible wimps if this is all they have been told they can be.

Are you grateful for your husband? Does he love you? Does he love your kids, play with them, coach their teams, read them good books, tuck them into their beds, and kiss them goodnight? Does he go to work each day to battle nobly in the corporate jungle?

Four years ago our family had a front-row seat to the disintegration of a family. It was heart wrenching and emotionally draining, and I was just the friend around the block, not the wife. To watch this family implode at such close range put any petty and selfish thoughts of mine back into perspective. You know the things I'm talking about, the things you and I pride ourselves on: the wet towel we dutifully pick up again, the toilets we clean, the underwear we fold, the meals we prepare, the sporting events we watch, the habits we overlook, the snoring we try to sleep through.

One particular day, upon retuning from my friend's house, I remember having to repent of my bad attitude toward my husband. I was shocked by all of the stupid, silly little things I had let myself hold onto. I remember crying and telling God how grateful I was for Davis and all of the stuff that aggravated me—especially that stuff because it meant he was home with me and the kids.

Here are a few things I do to show my appreciation for Davis.

Chase and Be Caught

Davis and l love to chase each other around the house. As the pursuit ensues, I might duck into a hallway or closet and let myself get caught. The kids love to watch.

We laugh and kiss while they point, snicker, and take pictures. By doing this, we are saying to them that this is what marriage looks like, this is what you do after all those years together, you still chase each other around the kitchen island. I believe that we are laying a foundation for their marriages when they see us still crazy in love with each other.

Write Notes

We write notes to each other. Sometimes they're little notes scribbled on scraps of paper. Sometimes they're carefully written in store-bought cards, sometimes transmitted via e-mail. They are widely varied in their content—personal, funny, sexy, serious, apologetic, a scripture, a challenge, a question, a request. Sometimes they are hand delivered, while on other occasions we enlist the kids to make the delivery, which they love. Now and then they are mailed—everyone loves receiving mail. Sometimes they are "found" or publicly posted on a mirror, chalkboard, or wall. They always tell of a love still growing, still committed, still passionate.

Take Walks

We love taking walks together. We'll walk early in the morning while the birds are singing, late at night when the whippoorwill is calling, at the beach with the tide and waves rolling. We walk around our neighborhood as others go about their lives, hand in hand, side by side. We walk, we talk, we unwind, we process, we vent, we debrief, we laugh, and we share.

Sometimes we walk in silence, thinking through something individually. But we are together. Walking has become symbolic of our life together. Some of our walks have been painful, some insightful. Others have been draining, and some invigorating. Each of them is about spending time together. We can't go out to eat at a restaurant every week, but we can take a walk almost every day.

Go Out on Dates

A date with my husband still makes my heart beat faster. Oh, how I love to go out with my beloved! It doesn't have to be fancy. Just something about being alone, only the two of us, makes my heart sing. We have done a variety of things on our dates. We have gone out for ice cream or coffee. We have eaten at nice restaurants and fast-food establishments. We have gone to see a movie and the occasional live performance. We have gone alone, and we have gone with friends. We have gone out in the morning and late at night. We set no rules. There is just one objective: being together.

Right now our favorite place to go is a particular Italian restaurant in town. We like to sit at the food bar, which overlooks the kitchen where the cooks are preparing the meals. It's great fun to watch the controlled chaos, and sometimes they give us free samples of the dishes they are preparing. We have an absolute blast. We share the crab cakes and olive oil with herbs. We sit really close together. Davis whispers in my ear and holds my hand. We don't really want to leave, but eventually the time comes. We take home lots of leftovers, which is the kids' favorite part.

Often on our dates we will reminisce about our journey. We'll talk about how we first met, what we first thought, what we did in those early days. Most often we talk about our dreams and hopes for the days to come.

Pray and Study Together

It's a cliché because it's true: The couple that prays together stays together. Prayer is at the very heart of enriching a marriage. There is nothing that will bind your hearts quite like time on your knees together—not a conversation, a walk, a note, a gift, a vacation, an act of service, not even sex. When we get down on our knees together, at the foot of the throne of Grace, that is where bonding occurs. There are issues, confessions, repentance, anxiety, excitement, and emotion revealed through prayer together. When Davis and I are on our faces before God, we are laid bare. There is a revealing of the soul that we share, a point of vulnerability and humility that brings us closer. Our hearts, our hurts, our pains, and our concerns are exposed in a safe way, and the masks and layers of artificial interaction are removed.

How Can I Serve You Today?

I once finished a Bible study by Elizabeth George that gave me a profound but simple takeaway I still use today: Serve your husband. I was reminded that Davis, like any man, has lots of pressure on him to provide, protect, and

lead the family. I came up with a trouble-free and unde-
manding question that I would sincerely asked him on
the occasional morning. I simply asked, "What can I do
to serve you today?" His natural response early on was a
pat one: "Nothing. I'm good." Pretty soon, he realized
I was serious, and he started thinking of some real and
practical answers. After all, we all could really benefit
from having someone serve us sometimes. Yes, being a
man, there were times when he could only think of one
thing. But you know what? That really was what served
him well at the time, with all the battles he was facing
that particular week.

If you ask the question often enough, your husband
will come up with a list of other practical needs he has.
Sometimes Davis was ready with a short list of easy er-
rands or phone calls that would lighten his load. These
little acts of service, given with a cheerful heart, proved
to be big deposits in my man's emotional and relational
bank account.

Serve your spouse. I can tell you from firsthand experience, what goes around comes around. This will up the
ante on serving one another intentionally and thinking of

the other person before yourself (Romans 12:10), which is a beautiful and biblical approach to enriching your life and marriage.

Blessing the Next Generation

My parents set a good example. Dad would come up behind Mom in the kitchen while she was working and snuggle her. He would whisper in her ear and give her love pats, and she would giggle in response. He always spoke to her softly and lovingly. When he was out of town, they would mail love notes to each other. I grew up thinking, *This is what love looks like.*

My childhood was not without its trials. We moved often, once overseas. I saw my parents work through conflict, loss, financial problems, sickness, pressure, and stresses of all kinds. They always looked to God and held each other's hands. That is how they made it. And that is where I learned how marriage was done.

The marriage that Davis and I share hasn't been without its challenges. None are. When a marriage seems flawless, it's simply because its flaws are better concealed than those in other relationships. Every marriage has its trials. But when our covenant has been made with God, He is always there to provide strength, grace, and forgiveness. He never leaves us, not ever. Sure, one spouse can choose to abandon God, but God never abandons His children.

Building a Firm Foundation

We know the power of expectations. When we lower our expectations, the actual results will almost always follow suit. In the best-selling book *Love and Respect*, Emerson Eggerichs asserts that the primary thing married men need is "respect" and the primary thing married women need is "love." He's right. Men need women to respect them as providers, as leaders, as fathers, as heads of their homes. They need their wives to hold them up in prayer, to encourage them, and to be willing to follow them as they follow God. It's no good being a leader when no one is following. To lead without followers is like cooking when no one is there to eat. It's like getting dressed up with nowhere to go. I really believe men *want* to lead. By resisting their leadership, we can tear down our houses with our own hands. On the flip side, by following their lead we can validate their headship, resulting in blessings for ourselves and our marriages—all of which will ultimately grab hold of a child's heart in a life-changing and God-glorifying way.

HEART CHECKUP

1. Describe your parents' marriage. What was great about it, and what do you wish had been different? What are some ways you can clearly see that their relationship has influenced your own marriage?

2. How would you like to see your own marriage improve? What are you personally willing to do to start making those changes?

3. Describe the kind of marriage you would like your children to one day experience. How are you helping to prepare them now for those relationships? How are you praying for them and their future spouses?

4. What interactions and habits in your marriage are examples worth imitating? What are some interactions and habits in your marriage that are not worth imitating?

5. What is one thing you could do today for your spouse that could make all the difference in his or her day?

Chapter 3
A: Accept Your Children

*In all my prayers for all of you, I always pray with joy . . . being
confident of this, that he who began a good work in you will carry
it on to completion until the day of Christ Jesus.*
Philippians 1:4–6

I still remember what it was like to take the at-home
pregnancy test, waiting in anticipation for confirmation
of a coming child. I was excited, almost giddy. Davis and
I had been married three years, and our future was so
bright.

This was not the case for a slave woman who lived
3,400 years ago under the tyranny of the Egyptians. The
crack of the overseer's whip was a daily, all-too-common
reminder of the hopelessness of Jochebed's plight. Exhaustion was her constant companion. She was not
dismissed from the work because of the demands of her
roles as wife or mother. No, she had to work double-
duty: slave by day, servant by night. Then there was the
emotional toll of watching her husband and children

labor under the endless demands of the slave drivers. Jochebed found herself praying, even though she wasn't sure anyone was listening. She couldn't seem to stop herself from crying out to the God of her fathers.

Then the unthinkable happened: She realized she was pregnant. *Surely not. No, not now. Please God, please don't make me watch another of my children suffer.*

Accidents or Blessings?

The *A* in our HEART acrostic is "Accept Your Children." This seems simple enough. You might even be tempted to skip this chapter, thinking you have this down already. But stick with me. Just as there is "supportive" and then there's *supportive*, there is "acceptance" and then there's *acceptance*. Your kids know the difference even if you don't. We may think we've accepted our children and all their uniqueness, but they know better.

Maybe you've heard parents introduce their kids something like this: "This is David, our oldest. Next is Martin, then Brad. And this is Joey, our Oops-we-thought-we-were-done son." This is followed by tense chuckles. Not so bad, you say? What about Joey? Does he join in the laughter? How secure does he feel? How wanted? How loved?

I remember a woman telling me the story—in front of her grown son—about how, after she found out she was pregnant with him, she walked up and down the stairs hoping to lose the pregnancy because she couldn't stand the thought of having another baby. *Ouch!* For what it's worth, this young man still doesn't know Christ.

Let's face it, our twenty-first-century society simply does not place a high value on children. Just look around. Some of the indicators are subtle and others are glaring, while some are shocking and others tragic. Yet, for the most part, these signs of rejection are not only legal, they are encouraged.

It's no wonder then that people gawk in wonder when I'm out with my kids and we're having a great time, laughing and enjoying each other. Some people cannot fathom the possibility that a mother can live with seven children and still *like* them. One man actually told me one day at the store that all these couldn't possibly be my kids—he said I was having entirely too much fun with them. What an unfortunate commentary on our world that it doesn't seem normal for a parent to enjoy her kids!

Consider the proliferation of daycare centers in our neighborhoods. The message is clear: By and large, as a society, we value our careers and our stuff more than our kids. Relationships with our children are relegated to weeknights and weekends. The lion's share of our time is devoted to our true priorities, our true treasures—jobs, homes, cars, clothes, PCs, iPhones. Stuff.

Oh, it's not that American culture doesn't like children. We love them—that is, until they are no longer cute. Alas, cute grows up. Cute throws up. Cute matures into the teen years with its acne, driving, debates, dates, and hormones. I can't tell you how many times I've been told, "Just wait until they're teenagers!" But no matter what people think or want to believe, you can't have kids without getting the whole package. Cute and cuddly grows up to become independent and sometimes testy.

Sure, the teenage years can be like the rest of life— hard. But hard is not unbearable. Hard is not the impossible. Hard is not the end. It's just hard. This brings us to God's point of entry. The hard place is where we most need Him, the place where He likes to show off.

The Biggest Show-off

Did you know that the God of the universe likes to show off? He does! And He's very good at it. Think of all the impossible, dead-end situations we read about in the Bible, the times when there seemed to be no way out, the times when a miracle was the only answer. God came through every time.

The first thing that comes to mind when I think of miracles is a baby. Have you looked at a baby lately? My oldest is now nineteen, and my youngest just turned six. But I can still remember when they were little. I can still picture those tiny toes, chubby fingers, soft ears, bright eyes, and shoulders covered with peach fuzz. The smallest among us are the greatest blessings—the physical representations of answered prayers. Jochebed had prayed for deliverance for her people, the Hebrews, and guess what? She gave birth to the deliverer! How's that for answered prayer?

Could it be that you or I have given birth to an answer to prayer? *That* will make you think. What are you urgently praying for? Godly government leadership?

A cure for cancer? Are you praying for a new generation of dedicated homeschool families? Missionaries to take the good news to the lost? Are you praying for the movie industry to portray more Christian themes? Fashions to become more modest? Advertisers to have more integrity? On a more personal note, is there a relative for whom you have prayed to receive Christ as Lord and Savior?

It's possible that the answers to some of these prayers are already here in the form of a child, a teenager, or a young adult. Are the answers to these prayers growing up under your roof? Which answer to prayer did you eat breakfast with this morning? With which answer did you worship God on Sunday? To which answer did you teach a new math concept today? Perhaps the answer to your prayers is just learning to sit up or use a cup? Did your "answer" skin a knee yesterday? Lose a tooth? Break an arm?

All through history, God has been sending little miracles to do His bidding, and always just in time. Noah, Abraham, Joseph, Moses, Joshua, Caleb, Gideon, Elijah, Samuel, David, Jeremiah, Isaiah, Daniel, and the rest of the prophets were all sent at a specific time in history in order to fulfill a specific purpose to glorify the Father. Mary and Joseph were born on a collision course with their appointed destiny to be the earthly parents of the Son of God. Elizabeth had longed to be a mother for so long, and when it was finally time, John the Baptist didn't miss his cue.

And, of course, the timing of Christ's arrival was perfect. The Gospel of John mentions the importance of timing over and over as when Jesus slips through the crowd on several occasions because "His time had not yet come."

For Such a Time as This

Review the stories leading up to the arrival of these particular mighty men and women as babies, and you will notice that most of them did not arrive under "ideal" circumstances. Noah was born at what the Bible describes as a wicked time. A quiet and righteous man who didn't have children till he was 500 years old, Noah's life took a sudden wild turn, and he became a laughingstock among his neighbors for the next hundred years while he built a large boat in his front yard.

Gideon was in hiding, threshing wheat in a wine press, while the people lived in fear of the Midianites.

Ruth's life was different from what she probably hoped for—she found herself a widow, moving to a foreign country with her depressed mother-in-law.

Jeremiah, called the weeping prophet, was persecuted at every turn and from a pretty young age. No one liked what he had to say, and he lived in constant danger.

Daniel was taken into captivity, perhaps as early as thirteen years of age.

Hosea was told to marry an adulterous woman with whom he had children, but who would not remain faithful.

Mary was told she had found favor in God's eyes. Yet in the eyes of the community where she lived . . . well, the look in their eyes was not favorable. Joseph didn't fair much better. He must have drawn jeers and tacky comments about his young bride from friends and family.

John the Baptist made his home in the desert, which couldn't have been the most welcoming or comfortable of living conditions.

Oh, the heartbreak of their respective mothers. The

timing must have seemed bad from the world's perspective. The tears they must have cried, the prayers they must have offered, the faith they must have exhibited. All of these men and women represented the radical yet understated hand of God—the hand we so often search for and so consistently miss. Each of these children represented tangible answers to prayer and God's faithfulness to His people. God used every one to reveal Himself to His people and to us. Each one was faithful in carrying out his or her task as appointed by God. And each started with a mother's acceptance.

The Son of Jochebed

Moses was born under a death sentence. Pharaoh had decreed that every male Hebrew child was to be killed (Exodus 1:22), so what was a mother to do? Incredibly, Jochebed wove a basket, covered it with pitch, placed her baby inside, then set it adrift, hoping against hope that it might float to a "safe" place. Did she have a chance to take the basket out for a test float? Was the first time that basket came in contact with the Nile's water when it was full of her precious child?

Did baby Moses drift in and out of sleep, his "cradle" rocking with the river's flow? Did he cry while older sister, Miriam, tried to quiet him from the bank? What did *she* see that day? Were there close calls? Were there soldiers? Dangerous currents? Animals? Or was it an unusually, almost surprisingly peaceful and quiet day along the riverbank?

Would you consider this act by Moses' mother to be representative of her acceptance of him or rejection? Was this a simple act of faith or of desperation? Had Jochebed accepted that she had done all she could do and simply placed her child into God's hands? Whatever the answers are to these questions, you can be certain she prayed. And her prayers were answered.

Real Acceptance, Real Change

Genuine acceptance of our kids means a radical change of perspective—a paradigm shift. It means seeing our children as gifts from the hand of the living God. It means realizing these kids were *not* sent by God to drive us crazy. Isn't that good news?

There were times when I thought I was doing penance for all of the shenanigans I pulled in childhood by giving birth to carbon copies of myself. You know what I'm talking about. I was that child who put my parents through the wringer. I was that strong-willed child who threw herself on a hardwood bedroom floor in rebellion at the tender age of twelve months! I was the one who always demanded to know *why*. I tested every rule, debated every decision, and pushed every limit. I was the child whose parents surely thought, *I hope you have kids like yourself someday!*

And indeed I have. My oldest, Charles, began challenging our authority at the age of eighteen months. I was naive enough to think that this meant we were going to get the terrible twos over with early. Wrong! We were merely *starting* early. Charles required a tight and short leash from an early age.

I remember one particular night at the end of a very long day when nothing had gone right. All the toys had been confiscated, tears had been shed, punishment administered, and my patience worn to a thread. That day I wasn't sure I was cut out for this whole motherhood thing. Davis arrived home to find us both happy to see him. To me, Davis represented a break—second shift, if you will. To our son, he represented a new and fresh challenge. It didn't take long for Davis to appreciate just how long my day had been.

That evening, I called my mother. When she picked up, I didn't even say hello—I just started apologizing. "I'm sorry, I'm sorry, I'm sorry, I'm sorry!" I was crying, suddenly grateful for all her years of loving me in spite of myself.

My mom had accepted me as a child, strong will and all. She did not try and change who I was. Instead, she set out to properly direct this part of my design to be used for God's glory. A great encouragement to me through the years, my mom taught me the importance of keeping an eternal focus while bringing every part of my being into submission to God's will.

Wired for His Use

My first two children—both boys—are complete opposites. Charles is a microwave, and my Anderson is a crock pot. Those first few years were crazy. I was trying to slow one down and speed the other up, to get one to be more even and the other to be more varied.

Think about it. If you cook chicken in a microwave oven, it might get done but not be edible. It will likely end up tasting like rubber. If a surgeon does his work like a microwave, he can be in and out in one minute, but end up with a dead patient because he rushed through the procedure. Microwave kids are in constant motion and easily distracted. They are able to do many things but lack consistent focus. When they *do* focus, it's a red-hot laser focus, which can inflict harm if misdirected yet can produce wondrous results if handled carefully by a trained professional.

By contrast, if you cook your chicken in a crock pot, it will be done and tasty, even though the process takes much longer. As a surgeon who performs his work like a crock pot will be extremely thorough, marveling over the many fascinating aspects of anatomy while in the midst of surgery As a result, surgery may take twice as long, but the stitching will be a thing of beauty, a work of art. Like a Timex watch that "takes a licking and keeps on ticking," crock pot kids sometimes need to be told to go outside and take a break. Otherwise, they will keep their noses to the grindstone and work all day and all night, rarely coming up for air.

Figuratively speaking, I turned both my boys upside down and removed their back panels, confident that one or both had faulty wiring and I was going to be able to fix them. I was sure God had messed up. I was going to rewire them to be completely compliant and obedient. I wanted the kind of kids that would make me look good (and feel good). Friends and neighbors would think I was a great mother who had it all together, and I liked that idea.

But Charles and Anderson were not sent to bring *me* glory. They were created to bring glory to God. Instead of resisting their bents—their original wiring—I needed to honor the way God had wired them. I needed to pray for Him to reveal His plan and purpose for their lives so I could raise them "in the way [they] should go" (Proverbs 22:6) so they could one day fulfill what He had planned for them.

That's not to say our kids come to us perfect. Oh no. There are things they need to work on. What it means is that they do not come to us "broken." We need to teach them who they are in Christ and then help them identify what God has called them to do. We need to help prepare them to glorify God.

When we attempt to rewire our children, we are actually rejecting them, even if we do not verbalize it. They can sense it. They feel it. Of course, we know not to tell a child we wish he were more like so-and-so, but if we're not careful, we can easily communicate this same negative message by our actions when we ignore or resent their strengths.

Our enemy, our children's enemy, is not content with the fact that we all have our weaknesses. He also wants to undermine our strengths. It is essential that we study our children and ask God to show us who these kids are for His glorious purpose. We need to learn their strengths and weaknesses so that we can equip them to be on guard, stand firm, and not grow weary in doing good.

God has a plan for our kids, though we might not have a clue what it is. There are days when I'm on my face begging God for just a *glimpse* of His plans for them because I'm at the end of my rope for the day—and it's only ten o'clock in the morning. No matter how difficult my hardest day is, God has a plan, and I can allow His peace to rule simply by resting in His plan. That's good news for all of us.

Sent Right on Time

Your kids were sent right on time, on purpose, "for such a time as this" (Esther 4:14). They are not randomly generated picks in the genetic lottery. God looked at your marriage, your life, your family, and your relationship with Him and decided to send each specific child to you, uniquely designed to bless your family. He sent these children to your home as tools to mold you and the other members of your family.

The birth order of your kids is also on purpose. Our middle child is Molly, and we make a point of telling her that this is a great place to be in the family. Tell your children what an awesome position God has placed them in. Affirm them in their position, the timing of their birth, and God's sovereign hand in it all.

What if you knew you were raising the next Billy Graham or Mother Teresa? What if you knew your child was the next Thomas Edison (who couldn't stay in school because of ADHD) or Marie Curie? What if you knew God's ultimate destiny for each of your children? How might you talk with them differently? Would you spend more time with them? Would you choose to talk about different things? How would your activities change? Would it change anything?

Physician, Heal Thyself

It is not your job to tear down your children. You are to build them up. Have you ever taken that little face in your hands and said, "I am so glad God sent you to our home. I am so excited about everything He has planned for your life. And I am so honored to help you in any way I can. You add joy to our home"?

There are times when all we want to do is read them the riot act. And if you're like me, you try and throw in enough Jesus to justify the venting. I have become convinced that what our kids really need is for us to pause and tell them how much we love them—and how much He loves them.

When my kids are caught in sin, they are usually quite clear on the idea that they've done something wrong. I've come to find out that what they need in that moment is not necessarily a speech. While it is appropriate to call them on their disobedience—through teaching, reproof, correction, and training in righteousness—what they need from me in that moment is to know that I am committed to them and that I'm going to stick by them no matter what. I let the Holy Spirit do the rest. Sometimes during these discussions my kids will tell me they just wish they could get this figured out. I might say, "Me too." Or I might say, "Look, I have issues too, and I want you to know that I am in this with you for the long haul. I've got your back. We're going to keep working this out." That is acceptance.

We must seek God first when it comes to molding our children, or we will make the mistake of molding them into our image instead of His. We will try to make them into what we want them to be for our pleasure and pride and not for the glory and praise of their heavenly Father. (It's easy to get snagged in the trap of wanting our kids to make us look good. This culture is full of parents living vicariously through their children.)

The first thing to do when you think you detect

something in our child that you think needs changing or refining is to look in the mirror. Is the character flaw you see in your child an imitation of our own sinfulness? Is it a simple case of "monkey see, monkey do"? I remember one day yelling to the kids about how they needed to stop yelling at each other. Yikes! I was teaching them by my own bad example what I didn't want them to do. This concept is the premise for my first book, *Soundbites from Heaven*, in which I discussed the idea that often the things we say to correct our children's behavior are the very things God would like to say to us.

This self-examination might bring you to a critical intersection. It might be that you find yourself confronted with an opportunity to make some changes in your own life, in your own character, and in your own attitudes. At that juncture, you get to work with your kids, grow with your kids, pray with your kids, and experience grace with your kids. I have done this many times. I've had to ask forgiveness from all my kids on occasion. When I do, I ask them to pray for me while I make some changes. This has been especially true with my first son, who was born at a time when I had given my heart to the culture and not to Christ. Sadly, I have seen in him attitudes that I know are there because I taught him so well. I have asked for grace from him and from God. God is faithful, and I am confident that He will do His perfect work through my imperfect parenting.

I have found that the best way for me to deal with sin in the lives and hearts of my kids is to take them back to God and His Word. First I remind them of who He is—their heavenly Father and the Maker of heaven and earth. I recount all that He has mercifully and graciously done on their behalf. Then I show them what God has to say in His Word regarding their sin. Sometimes I have them write down various scriptural references to the sin and its consequences. After they write the scriptures, we discuss them and pray together for the Holy Spirit to do His mighty work in their hearts and give them strength to live obediently. Frequently, these sins are clear patterns of behavior—character flaws, if you will. In such cases, I encourage them to commit the verses to memory and recite them at times of temptation or difficulty. We all have weaknesses we struggle with, and it's important to teach our kids how to overcome by the Word of the Lord.

What Acceptance Does Not Mean

Acceptance does not mean permissiveness. Accepting your children does not mean that they get whatever they want, wherever they want, whenever they want. Your kids do not need you to take a hands-off approach to their lives in the name of God's sovereignty and providence. Acceptance means you recognize that God intentionally sent these specific children to your family, that He has plans for you as their parent, for them as your children, and for both of you as *His* children. It doesn't mean trying to fashion them into your image or mold them into someone you want them to be for selfish reasons. Rather, acceptance means seeking His will and purpose for each child He places in your care. It means accepting and enjoying each one as a providential gift and a blessing from a Holy God, trusting that He will continue the good work He began by sending them to you and carry it through to completion (Philippians 1:6). But don't use your trust in Him as an excuse for passive parenting.

In fact, choosing not to discipline your children in the name of acceptance would be abdicating the responsibility you have been given as a parent. We are admonished to train up our children in the way they should go (Proverbs 22:6). This training is not without discipline. The Bible teaches that "foolishness is bound up in the heart of a child," but "the rod of discipline will remove it far from him" (Proverbs 22:15, NASB). Accepting our children does not mean approving of their foolishness. In fact, we are obligated to drive out their foolishness even more intentionally because we believe that God has made them for a unique purpose that does not allow for selfishness or foolishness.

Well-disciplined children are not only prepared for God's call and work in their lives, but they are also enjoyable to spend time with. Children who obey and honor their parents are a pleasure to have in your presence. God wants us not only to accept our children but also to enjoy our children. I remember thinking that I would be willing to accept my kids if they would just do what I wanted them to do. This was before I took into account what God's plan might be for them. Back then it was all about me, and if they would only do what I wanted them to do—i.e., make me look good—*then* I could enjoy them.

I was way off base.

During this parenting journey, you and I are going to be challenged to accept some aspects of God's plans that are more than a little uncomfortable. Our children are each one-of-a-kind creations. God's Word says that they were known by God as He formed them in the hidden places (Psalm 139:15), that they are created in Christ Jesus for good works which He has prepared in advance for them to do (Ephesians 2:10). Accepting your kids also means accepting, embracing, and fulfilling your role in the molding and directing process. He has a plan for how your particular personality, experiences, temperaments, gifts, and perspective will work in the lives of your children to prepare them for all He has planned. When parenting seems hard or downright impossible, and you're certain you've messed things up beyond repair, don't forget that you serve the great Redeemer and all of that stuff in your life that you regard as junk can and will be used by God for good (Romans 8:28). He works through it all, redeeming it all, and turning it all around when you trust in His providence and intervention.

The Potter's Apprentice

Have you ever watched a potter work? It's an amazing process, really. The clay doesn't look like much at first. It's certainly not worth much. It's just a lump, colorless and unshapely. Yet the potter sees something in the clay. He has a vision for what it could be, what it might be, if it will submit to the pressure of his hands as it turns on the wheel. Even as the clay begins to take shape in the eyes of the onlooker, it still appears far from anything useful. Yet the potter patiently works, getting filthy as he patiently attends to the details of the clay form. He may use tools to assist him in shaping and decorating his creation. In the end, once the spinning stops, the clay has taken shape but it is not yet stable for use. Now it's time for the furnace. In the intense heat, the clay is tested and proven. On the other side of the oven, the creation cools until it is ready to fulfill the function for which it was designed.

Our journey with our kids is not just about disciplining and training them. It is also about *our* discipline and training. I know that I have done some major growing up with my kids, yet I still have far to go. My character is constantly being molded into the image of Christ and is slowly being perfected. Parenting is clearly not at all about me, and yet it is about me: ˙God is using this opportunity not just to prepare my children for His calling, but also to break me, mold me, and use me as an instrument of righteousness for His name's sake—if I will let Him.

Outside the Box

Accepting God's will for the lives of our kids means thinking outside of the box—way outside. The world's wisdom says that there is a certain prescribed method by which children determine and accomplish their goals, yet God's path will probably not be conventional, traditional, or rational to the critics. God's wisdom is foolishness to man (1 Corinthians 1:18). As we defer to His wisdom to raise our children well, we must look for ways to support and encourage God's call on their lives. We must give them opportunities to explore and experience God's faithfulness, provision, and affirmation of His plans for their future.

I don't know why I thought Charles's or Anderson's

post-high-school education would be "traditional," given how non-traditional the previous thirteen years had been. Charles is such a unique person, and I know that God has uncommon plans for him. I shouldn't have been surprised that the path God had in store for him would be way outside the box. My first step in being able to faithfully consider God's plan for Charles and the dreams God has given him for the next few years is what I have been saying all along: I need to accept him as he was uniquely designed by God for His purposes.

Several years ago I read a report regarding how often children heard the words "I love you." I don't remember all the statistics, but it was sad that in these United States many children rarely hear these important words—foundational, life-giving words. These are the words by which children first begin to build trust. These are the words that best communicate a parent's acceptance of the child. But as important as those three words are, there are three words that are more important: *God loves you.*

A couple of years ago, during a television interview, I was asked what I would most want my children to remember me saying to them? My impromptu answer surprised me: "The thing I want my children to hear more than anything else is not that I love them, though that would be a tight second. The thing I want my kids to hear more than anything else is that the God of the universe loves them." That is the truth I want to ring in their ears long after they leave home. Those words will minister to their souls in powerful, providential, and eternal ways.

God loves you.

These words will teach your children that there is a God, He created them, and He has definite plans for them.

HEART CHECKUP

1. What are some ways you have experienced rejection in your own life? (Remember, all of these come from the father of lies!)

2. Are there characteristics of your children you find difficult to accept? If so, what are they? Pray about these specifically and ask to see God's perspective about these areas of your children's lives.

3. Are there things about your children you're personally embarrassed about? If so, what are they? Pray about these specifically and ask to see God's perspective about these areas of your children's lives.

.

Chapter 4
R: Release Them to God

Sons are a heritage from the Lord, children a reward from him. Like arrows in the hands of a warrior are sons born in one's youth. Blessed is the man whose quiver is full of them. They will not be put to shame when they contend with their enemies in the gate.
Psalm 127:3–5

She wanted one thing: a son. Desperate, exhausted, and sobbing she cried out to God. She begged, pleaded, and talked to herself. Then she talked to God again, praying for the answer that eluded her, that drove her, that consumed her. On her knees and her face, she prostrated herself, not caring who might see or hear and especially not caring what they might think.

That is how Eli found Hannah. Eli, the last of the judges of Israel and high priest, he did the same thing any of us would do: He jumped to a conclusion and judged her on the spot, accusing her of being intoxicated (1 Samuel 1:13–14). Compassion? He failed that test.

Without sympathy or sensitivity he spoke, assuming he knew and understood. He didn't join her and get on his knees, nor did he try to comfort her with a hug or even look her in the eye. Hannah was pouring her heart out, and Eli stomped on it.

Nevertheless, God granted Hannah's request, and she goes on to provide us an example of releasing our children to God. She fully understood the blessing she had been given. Her son was a gift, and it would be an honor and privilege to raise him in the fear and the admonition of the Lord. Samuel was merely on loan from the moment of his conception. Hannah knew what her son was called to do, and she gladly took on the role of preparing him for that purpose, training him for work in the temple as Eli's assistant.

They Are Not Ours

These kids we refer to as ours are not ours. They are His. God has graciously loaned them to you and me at this time and for His glory. Let that soak in for a moment: *Your children are not yours.* Initially, this can be a terrifying thought, but I believe it is ultimately liberating. It's a simple truth but a difficult one: They are His, and He has assigned each child specifically to you and your family for the purpose of living and acting according to His perfect plan.

It's fine to want things for your children, to want the best for them. After all, you love them. So often I hear parents say, "All I want is for my kids to be happy." Really? What if their happiness means making your life miserable? What if criminal behavior makes them happy? What if breaking God's law makes them happy? Is "happiness" really the standard we want to set for our kids?

The desires we have for our kids must move way beyond their earthly happiness. We must instead be focused on giving our children the joy of the Lord. We must recognize our children's highest calling is to glorify the one true God and enjoy Him forever. We must therefore release them to follow God with reckless abandon and to seek His plan for their lives. We must let go of our own selfish dreams for them.

Only by following God, obeying Him, and honoring Him in all they say and do can our children ever hope to know real, genuine, lasting joy. That's what it means to train up a child in the way he should go—to help him go in the way that God directs.

We are to constantly and consistently point our children toward God and His sovereign will and purpose for their lives. We should be asking questions like, "What do you think God's direction is for your life?" "What talents do you think He has given you?" "How do you think you might best serve Him?" "What draws your heart to God?" "Are you on the right path?" "How can I help you?"

God has merely entrusted our children to us, and only for a time. Many of us seem to think this means we get to keep them until either the parent or the child dies. But I believe there is a limited period of time we are given to train and disciple our children. Ideally, we should want our children to experience all that God has planned for them instead of wanting them to become people of our own construction for our own glory.

Perhaps this seems obvious to you—a walk in the park—until it comes time to release your kids into His care, for the fulfillment of His purpose, His plan, and His will. In the end, it comes down to a trust issue. It's not a question of whether or not you trust your kids. The question is this: Do you trust God?

This Gets Easier, Right?

Who am I that He would trust me with these seven kids? Sometimes it takes my breath away. It overwhelms me. This parenthood thing has not progressed the way I thought it would. It's much harder and occasionally seems to get harder daily.

I figured the most difficult days were behind me once they were all sleeping through the night, when they were potty trained, when they could buckle themselves in the car, when they could make themselves a peanut-butter-and-jelly sandwich. After all, I should be more rested, right? I should have more time to go on dates with my husband, more time to study God's Word, more time to organize my day, do laundry, and keep the house in order. Wrong.

I didn't know these little people would silently process life all day long then want to discuss it with me late into the night. No one warned me that these discussions only become more intense and the decisions more personal as they grew older.

I raised them "out of the box" (a.k.a. homeschooling) and they are not going to be magically drawn to a life back "in the box" where everything is safe, simple, and close to home. It doesn't work that way. What I have found is that when you raise kids to think of heavenly things, to consider God, to love Him, and to seek Him—well, then anything could happen. When you teach them about God's faithfulness, sovereignty, and grace; when you don't rain on their parades with words like "too much," "too far away," "too big," or "too hard"; then they begin to believe that anything is possible. Your kids were meant to change the world. Think of it: young men and women dreaming great dreams for His glory. Isn't that what this is all about?

We Already Know

Hannah's goal in training Samuel was clear: prepare him to work in God's house. Do you suppose she raised him differently than other mothers were raising their sons? You bet she was. You see, Hannah was focused. She had a purpose, a perspective. She knew what she was trying to accomplish. She wanted to give back to God, to make good on her promise.

You might argue that it was easy for her know how to train Samuel because she knew what he was destined to become. Well, so do we! It's all there in black and white and, in some New Testaments, red. You and I know what our kids are destined to be: sons and daughters of the King, servants of the Most High, leaders of the next generation, visionaries of what He might do. In fact, we know just as much as Hannah knew.

Aren't we called to raise our kids to love, honor, and obey God? Aren't we training them to seek God and point others to Him? Aren't we encouraging our kids to serve Him, to offer their bodies as living sacrifices, and to see their bodies as temples of the Holy Spirit? It doesn't matter if they grow up to become doctors or lawyers, mothers or nurses, accountants or diplomats, hairstylists or car dealers. They are to be prepared to honor God in whatever they say and do.

Like Hannah, we can prepare our kids for their "whatever." Mind you, this is not the world's flippant, passive, or lazy "whatever." Just the opposite. This "whatever" is more like a huge blank check on which you sign your name and wait for God to fill in the rest. It's total surrender. It's a growing, intimate, passionate pursuit of God's perfect plan without our sinful and selfish limitations. It is a holy "whatever." A sacrificial "whatever." A "whatever" of epic proportions with life-changing power.

However, sometimes we get distracted by the details and miss the cross for the forest. We get wrapped up in chasing after achievement for our children according to the world's standards: SAT scores, Ivy League schools, business card titles, 401(k) plans, vacations, and so on. We forget the standard set on Calvary. Instead of sacrificing ourselves, we crucify Christ all over again as we worship at the world's altars and at the feet of its idols.

Hannah refused to do so. I am convinced that she focused and refocused herself on her purpose—on her promise. She set her jaw, determined to make good on the vow she had made. Friends, neighbors, and relatives were no doubt mystified by the intensity of her focus. "Why so serious?" they probably asked. "After all, he's only a child." But Hannah knew better. Sure, they made some really good points. She was probably grateful for the advice even though they couldn't understand. Because of them she laughed and enjoyed Samuel more than she would have otherwise.

I imagine Hannah was determined but also torn. When Hannah's husband went up to offer the family's annual sacrifice to the Lord, Hannah elected to stay behind. She said to her husband, "After the boy is weaned, I will take him and present him before the LORD, and he will live there always" (1 Samuel 1:22). I'm only guessing, but I think I might be able to make a case for Samuel being nursed longer than any other child in history. Like many of us, Hannah was trying to fill her heart with as many memories as it could possibly hold: the smiles, the first time he rolled over, the squeals of delight, the way his hair was ruffled in the morning, and the first time he said, "Momma." She would hold his hand while she nursed him, and his fingers would cling tightly to her own. Sometimes he would drift off to sleep as she sang to him, and she would caress his toes and his shoulders. He was beginning to get distracted now when it was time to nurse, and he could manage a cup just fine. Hannah couldn't make the sun stand still. It was almost time.

She wanted Samuel to remember her smile, so she saved her tears for moments when he was asleep or playing. And while the tears fell silently, she would pray. She wouldn't fight or wrestle with God on this one. She would release her child with anticipation and perhaps some dread, but clearly hoping and dreaming of the life he would lead apart from her. She would have peace in keeping her vow.

As I write this, the time has come for my oldest son to leave home. Where did the time go? Like Hannah, I had prayed for a son. I prayed that he would be a mighty man of God, and I promised to prepare him for whatever God had planned for him. In retrospect, mine was an innocent and naïve prayer. I didn't really have a clue what this would mean, what it would require, or how it would play out. Though Charles is much older than Samuel was when Hannah presented him to Eli, he still seems so young in my eyes.

Like Hannah, I knew this day would come, but I didn't always use this knowledge to my advantage. I've been impatient, demanding, and selfish. I was not as focused as I should have been on the task at hand, having become distracted by so many small issues that I lost count of them all. Too many days were wasted, too many opportunities lost, too many moments missed, and I struggle with feelings of defeat.

Praise the Lord that we serve the great Redeemer, for He makes all things new! As the day approached for Charles to move out, not only did I have to release him into the hands of God, but I also had to lay down my countless failures and shortcomings at the foot of the cross. The enemy crouches at the door of my heart, waiting desperately to discourage and oppress me with reminders of my sinful, imperfect track record as a homeschooling mother. As never before, I had to take every thought captive and make it obedient to the truth of God's Word (2 Corinthians 10:5), focusing my mind on what is true, right, noble, excellent, and praiseworthy (Philippians 4:8). To do so, I had to actively submit to God and resist the devil, knowing that he would flee from me (James 4:7).

So Many Distractions, So Little Time

As we train our children for Him we must keep our priorities straight. I humbly suggest we place the strongest emphasis on their relationship with God the Father, the Son, and the Holy Spirit. Our second priority should be to encourage their relationships with their parents, their siblings, and extended family and friends. Only after laying a firm foundation for these relationships should we concern ourselves with academic achievement. Yes, our children need to learn math, foreign language, writing, and science, and we must be diligent in teaching these subjects with excellence. My point is that we never teach these to the detriment of nurturing their relationship with their Creator and Savior.

We must take the time necessary to deal with character training and teaching Truth with a capital *T*. The other subjects can and must wait; there will be time to fit them in. We must put first things first. Seek first the kingdom of God and His righteousness (Matthew 6:33). Don't fall into the trap of replacing what should be our first love with mere academics (Revelation 2:4).

I believe the success of the modern homeschooling movement can largely be attributed to the blessing of God as He has honored those pioneering parents who chose to live by faith in Him and knowledge of His Word. God has blessed homeschooling families not only with remarkable parent-child relationships but also academically as parents sought Him first and put academics second. Many of these parents were unsure how to teach upper-level math, phonics, biology, or French, but they believed God was calling them to take back their kids from the public school system with its worldly, relativistic, anti-Christian agenda. They trusted the Lord to fill in the gaps.

These parents valued Christ-like character over mere head knowledge, recognizing that high standardized scores without character and integrity are largely worthless. They took God up on His fundamental promise that if we put Him first, "all these things will be added" to us (Matthew 6:33, NASB). This principle is clearly seen in Acts 4 when the apostles Peter and John are brought before the Sanhedrin. What sets these men apart from the crowd as they face an intimidating council that only recently sanctioned the crucifixion of the Son of God? Is it their collective degrees from "Jerusalem University" and the "Israel Institute of Higher Learning"? Is it their charisma? Their enthusiasm? The awards they won at local speech and debate tournaments? No, in verse 13 we are told that Peter and John were "unschooled" and "ordinary" men (or, as we like to say at our house, *home-schooled* and ordinary men).

What sets these men apart, according to this same scripture, is that Peter and John "had been with Jesus." That's the advantage I want my kids to have. The world is not in short supply of "smart" people. We have plenty of men and women who can manipulate numbers, create new products, or coordinate marketing strategies. But this world is short—way short—of people who have been with Jesus on an everyday basis, cultivating an intimate relationship with the Lord of lords.

We need to make it a priority to be with Jesus ourselves and to introduce our children to Jesus. Spend time walking together and discussing Jesus. Get to know Him, worship Him, trust Him, admire Him. Imagine what it will be like to meet Him. O that others would describe us and our kids as those who have been with Jesus! That's what will make a difference to a lost and dying world—not another perfect SAT score, another degree, or another accomplishment. Time spent with Him will make our faces to radiate His glory, goodness, and grace. That is what will make a difference.

With Much Prayer

As I mentioned in the introduction, when Davis and I attended our first homeschool conference the Lord providentially led us into a workshop led by Chris Davis. Chris spoke of these very ideas. He said that children were blessings on loan from God in order that we might train them up to serve Him. He outlined a prayer that has become so precious to me—I have prayed it over my children individually and as a group many, many times.

First, Chris suggested that we pray God would give them and us a vision for who they are and are meant to be for His kingdom. He emphasized the importance of emptying myself of any preconceived notions of I want the kids to be and seeking God's good and perfect will. As I have prayed this for my kids, God has been gracious to grant me glimpses of His plan through their gifts, talents, interests, and dreams. The children and I have had many discussions in which I start by asking, "What is God showing you lately?" There's usually a pause followed by measured words, as this is serious stuff. Life stuff. God stuff. I find that it encourages both of us to discuss the movement of the Father in our lives, our hearts, and our circumstances.

Second, Chris suggested we pray that God would equip us to equip them. Have you ever received a glimpse of what God is doing and been awestruck by the enormity of it all? Boy, I have! Sometimes it's happened when I was feeling overwhelmed by the task ahead. Sometimes it's happened when the mere funding of the task seemed "too much."

There have been times when the kids' God-given dreams appeared impossible from my perspective. I certainly didn't know how to help them learn Mandarin Chinese, Arabic, or computer animation. I had no training that made me feel equipped to teach debate or anatomy and physiology. Worldview? Apologetics? Surely these were "impossible" too.

But God…

There is that phrase again. He knows our every need, and as we bring them before Him in faith, He answers, He provides, and He supplies. As I think back on all He has done in my family, I simply *must* praise Him.

We have heard it said that He doesn't call the equipped, but that He equips the called. I have seen it myself. He does it when we aren't looking, when we don't get it, when we've thought it unnecessary, and when we least expect it. So often He works without any big "to-do," and tragically, we chalk it up to coincidence. Without great fanfare, He has provided camps, mentors, professionals, trips, opportunities, and all the extras that have helped to fashion my kids into what He has planned for them.

The third thing we need to pray for our kids is that they will remain pure mentally, emotionally, physically, and spiritually. These days impurity is celebrated in our culture. Magazines and television shows tout the escapades of the rich and famous and foolish. Their trysts and irresponsible behavior are written up with laud and admiration. Their faces adorn the covers of magazines, their private lives for sale. By contrast, purity is considered outdated, boring, and selfish. Those who are determined to keep their minds and bodies pure for the King's use are few and widely criticized.

Even in our churches, it has become vogue to take a walk on the wild side to develop one's "testimony." If only we could understand what God has redeemed us from, without our creative additions, it would cause us to gasp! Every single one of us already has a testimony. I am talking about the moment when we realized our sinful state, the seriousness of it, the penalty of death required for it, and our need of Christ's blood to cover it. We would all do well to remember that moment often—the moment we made the great exchange. This was the moment we repented of our sinful, selfish ways and accepted His love, grace, and salvation.

One thing that Chris Davis didn't mention that day, but that I have added to the prayer for my kids, has also become my most fervent request. I pray that Jesus would be "real" to my kids. By this I mean they will recognize and accept that truth—i.e., all that is real—is in Jesus.

When we recognize, accept, and embrace that God is real, everything changes. And I mean everything—the sunrise, the flower's bloom, the bird's song, the leaf's complexity, the child's laughter. It changes the cotton-candy sunset, the starry host, the full moon, and the owl's midnight call. God's "being" changes everything because it all showcases His glory, His creativity, His uniqueness, and His wonder. As the reality of His existence sweeps over us and causes our souls to steer toward Him, then the great I AM will profoundly affect our every decision, every thought, every dream, every hope, and every pursuit.

It is not enough for our kids to appreciate the masterful creation of God's hand, to merely and willingly credit Him with the colors, details, and harmony of it all. No, God wants us to experience creation as a profoundly personal expression of His love, of His desire to have a personal relationship with each of us.

I love sunflowers. I love their beauty and strength. They stand so straight and tall and bold, lifting their heavy heads toward the life-giving sun and following its path across the summer sky. A couple of years ago our family was walking through a particularly difficult time.

It was summer, which is usually my favorite time of year. But my senses were dulled because of our circumstances. Then one day, a very special day, we were driving home and there it was: a field of sunflowers, practically in our own back yard. I felt overwhelmed by God's personal touch on my life. He had brought me flowers—not in a vase or a box, but firmly planted in the earth—a beautiful bouquet of sunflowers as far as the eye could see.

I paused, and I wept. Those flowers reminded me of His awareness of our situation, even though I had felt alone. He was there. He was *real* to me in that moment, and it undergirded my faith, giving me a boost. A smile and a song came to my lips: "Oh Lord, my God, when I in awesome wonder consider all the worlds Thy hands have made . . ."

The Bible teaches that narrow is the path that God has set for us to follow (Matthew 7:13). This doesn't sound so bad until you look around to find yourself alone, or you come to a crossroads and find friendships divided by the choice, often over issues of holiness or purity. We need to pray that God, His Word, and His faithfulness, will guide the decisions our kids make at the inevitable intersections of life and that they will have faith in Him alone—the one, true, and living God.

Guard Your Vision

Have you dared to dream for your kids? I don't mean a specific dream like playing professional sports or performing at Carnegie Hall, but a dream that God would use your children mightily. Do you have a confidence and assurance that God has great plans for each and every one?

When my children were infants, as I rocked them or held them, I would say, "God loves you. He has big plans for you. Huge plans. World-changing plans!" When the kids grew older, I woke them each morning saying, "What might God do today to show you His love? He loves you so much!" When discipline was necessary, I would tell them, "You know, God loves you. He has big plans for you. World-changing plans. I can hardly wait to see what He has planned. I am praying for you."

Over and over I have told them of His love and taught them that He has a plan for their good and for His glory. We have dreamed together, imagined together, and prayed together. We have explored the possibilities. What might God do in their lives?

Once you and your children get a vision for what God has planned for them, you can be certain the enemy will not take this affront lying down. When your children embrace God's call to go wherever and whenever He directs, it's like painting a target on their backs. The enemy will seek to bring them down, and he is relentless.

Our enemy keeps tabs on those who pose a threat to him—anyone who desires to follow God with wholehearted devotion, who is committed to doing whatever God desires, is definitively a threat. The good news is the devil is not omniscient (all-knowing) like our heavenly Father, no matter what he would have you believe. However, the enemy does closely study your kids' strengths and weaknesses, and his appetite for bringing them down is insatiable. He is determined to steal, kill, and destroy. He plays dirty, and he never gives up.

The command to be "on guard" is expressed in Scripture many times. Our oldest son participated in Civil Air Patrol, the Air Force civilian auxiliary program. Throughout his training, the unit went on several encampments. One of the assignments for those weekends was guard duty. I remember when he came in from one such weekend and announced, "You know, that guard duty thing is really harder than it sounds!" And he was right! The admonition to be on guard is a call to action and alertness, not passivity.

In order to be on guard, you and your children must actively prepare your minds. We prepare our minds by setting them on things above—praying constantly and meditating on the truth found in creation and in God's Word. As you consider your eternal home in heaven, you will be energized and inspired for the task ahead. Once you enter the place of releasing your kids, relinquishing your rights to their lives, and releasing them into the Master's hands for His purpose and plan, you have entered an intense battle zone—the front lines you might say—so you had best be on guard. This is guerilla warfare where no rules apply, all bets are off, winner take all.

Many Are Called

Did you know there are many missionaries living right here in America, going every day to jobs they find unfulfilling, dreaming of going to far-off lands to preach the good news to the captives? Why are they here instead of in the mission field? For many, it's because their parents *didn't want* them to go. A foreign posting in a dangerous country? How dare they even *think* of taking our grand-kids so far away and putting them in harm's way.

Shame on us for holding on to our children like that. Remember, they are not ours.

My oldest daughter, Savannah Anne, wants to go to China to serve as a missionary. Yes, *that* China, the one halfway around the globe. God laid this on her heart at an early age. She has baked cookies, saved, planned, and prayed to go for several years, and who am I to stand in the way of God's calling?

Savannah Anne has a heart for children in the or-phanages of China. I can picture her now—a blonde in a sea of black hair, with a big beautiful smile, walking through an orphanage singing, "Jesus Loves the Little Children."

I am already praying for the strength to one day drive her to the airport and put her on a plane, not knowing if I will ever see her again this side of glory, but know-ing she is doing the will of the Father. I know she will be safer in the middle of God's will than she would ever be living across the street. God loves her more than I could ever possibly try.

I believe in a *big* God. I believe in a God who grants the desires of hearts yielded to Him—those who dream big, God-sized dreams. Consider for a moment some of the great men and women who dared to dream and ended up achieving amazing things for God's kingdom: Mother Teresa, Jim Elliot, Mary Slessor, William Carey, Amy Carmichael, and Adoniram Judson. They all had mothers who loved them and nurtured them, mothers who smiled at them and prayed for them. They had mothers who pointed them toward God and His Son, Jesus Christ; moms who nurtured their dreams, talents, and gifts; moms who dared to let them go to where He called them; moms who didn't settle for a life of ease but who prayed through the night watch; moms who dared to trust, who didn't shrink from their moment of testing by holding on to their sons or daughters too tightly; moms who encouraged and supported their dreams; moms who believed in a better world to come, in an eventual reunion, if not here, then at the throne of grace; moms who dared to give their children back to God for His service.

There are times I wonder if perhaps I've been holding on more to my kids than to my God. As a homeschooling mom, I have so much invested in these kids. We've battled through some tough stuff together. Let go? Are you kidding? Why would I do that? Because it would honor God.

Most of us would probably like it best if our kids moved next door after they've grown up. That's because our focus is on the here and now. But if we will dare to shift our focus to heaven, to eternity, then we will see we have forever together and that time here is really very short. We will see how sending them out into the world as young adults will benefit God's kingdom. We might even become a little excited to imagine what God might do, how He will faithfully provide, and what He will redeem in and through these world changers.

If we were to catch just a glimpse of what these children could do to impact the world for Christ, we would not only be liberated from our short-sighted plans for our kids and their futures, but we might even be rejuvenated for the task of raising and teaching them.

I ask again, what if you knew right now that you were raising the next Billy Graham? The next Mother Teresa? A future president of the United States? A Supreme Court Justice? Perhaps you are! Someone is. Why not begin to think outside the box and teach your kids to think outside the box? Why not start imagining now and begin an ongoing conversation with your children that starts with "What might God do?"

What might God do with a few good young men and women who are trained and committed and released to do whatever God has planned for them to do? What might God do with a generation prayed for, prayed over, and prayed with? What might God do with kids whose parents are dedicated to Him and His will first? What indeed? Picture it: your children ready, willing, and able to change the world. And couldn't the world use some real change right about now?

When I was a kid and mom took us to the library, I thought that the books were ours to keep. Borrowing was a difficult concept for me. Like the time a friend let me borrow her dress—I didn't want to give it back. I wanted to keep it. The other side of this coin was if I couldn't keep it, what was the point in taking care of it? It wasn't mine, so why should I care? Of course, I learned that's exactly why I should care. This is the core of the golden rule, that I should take care of it like I would want someone to take care of my things if I loaned them out. Being allowed to borrow something is a trust, a responsibility.

We need take care of our children as if they were our own while being ever mindful of the fact that, from the beginning, they were never ours to keep.

Release them to God. They are His, and He will take great care of them.

HEART CHECKUP

1. What lessons can you personally draw from the stories of Hannah and Jesus' mother, Mary?

2. Has God given you a vision for what He has planned for each of your children? How are you preparing them for the future God has planned for them?

3. How can having an eternal perspective on your children's life purpose impact what you choose to do today? Tomorrow? Next year?

4. What are some things you can begin praying about as you prepare yourself and your children for the time of their release into the world?

Chapter 5
T: Teach Them the Truth

These commandments that I give you today are to be upon your hearts. Impress them on your children.
Deuteronomy 6:6–7

Our culture is so full of lies that it's difficult to know where to start listing them. In generations past, the lies were of the back-alley, smoke-filled-room variety. These were lies that nearly everyone could identify, that almost everyone acknowledged as lies. Not so anymore.

Today's lies have graduated to respectability, having worked their way up through the ranks of "make-believe" and "funny stories." Over the course of a single generation, a generation that was distracted and oblivious to the danger, these lies became firmly entrenched. Not only are they now acceptable in our culture, but they're even considered reasonable, legitimate, common knowledge.

No one was standing guard, standing firm, or standing strong. The night watch was snoring as the enemy infiltrated the camp with stealthy cunning. They crept in quietly at first—in an interview, the lyrics of a song, a sitcom, a movie, a magazine article, a political campaign. Many of them snuck in under the guise of tolerance, and to many, these lies looked good. At worst, they might be shrugged off as merely personal preference.

Now these lies are no longer in stealth mode. They are overt, in your face, and startlingly confrontational, daring us to speak out publicly or resist their further advancement. Meanwhile, they are redecorating our town squares and courtrooms and rewriting our textbooks, our history, our heritage. So much has gone missing.

Where did it go? Who took it? When did it happen? It's time we woke up and opened our eyes.

The Dangerous Dance of Deceit

As a parent there are few things more frightening than seeing your child in danger, especially when you cannot quickly come to the rescue. Think of a mom standing at her kitchen sink and looking out the window to see her child chasing a stray ball that is heading towards the street and straight into the path of an oncoming car.

When our youngest son, Benjamin, was about two years old, he was playing on our front porch. I could hear him laughing, but he's always been such a happy child that I didn't think much of it. His delight continued until I just had to see what was amusing him so. I looked out the window and saw that Ben was pursuing a large, angry hornet. Ben chased it, and then it chased him. This was great fun, or so Ben thought. I figured it was only a matter of time before my son got stung. The hornet was clearly angry and anxious to make his point—literally.

Although he didn't get stung that day, Ben has since learned that hornets do not make very good playmates. Now that he's been stung, he is on guard. Now he can identify a hornet and steers clear.

Lies are very much like hornets. As young children, we might think that they are fun to chase or that it is fun to be chased. As adolescents, we might think it fun to catch them in a jar, just to prove we can. However, once stung, we learn there's a price for our daring and a penalty for "harmless" experimentation. Hornets sting, snakes bite, lions attack, and elephants charge. Lies are like wild animals—dangerous and unpredictable.

The Most Important Thing to Teach Your Children

If you had to name the number one thing we need to teach our kids, what would it be? How to handle money? How to communicate? How to earn a living? How to choose a spouse? The value of an education? Conflict resolution? Time management? The virtue of hard work? If there was only one thing we could pass on to our kids, to the next generation, what should it be?

Why does this question give us pause? Why isn't the answer obvious? Why doesn't the opportunity to teach it to our children excite and invigorate us? Why doesn't it challenge us, inspire us, or make us want to jump out of bed in the morning? It should. Because there is an answer to that question—a clear and concise answer. This answer has gone unchanged since the command was originally given in the Old Testament:

"These commandments that I give you today are to be upon your hearts. Impress them on your children. (Deuteronomy 6:6–7)

"Fix these words of mine in your hearts and minds. . . . Teach them to your children." (Deuteronomy 11:18–19)

He decreed statutes for Jacob and . . . commanded our forefathers to teach their children, so the next generation would know them. (Psalm 78:5–6)

Teaching our kids truth is the most important thing we can do or accomplish as parents. It's paramount that we give them knowledge and understanding of the one true and living God. This is the foundation upon which all other knowledge is built. If we focus on anything else, then we doom our children to lives of emptiness and hopelessness.

As followers of Jesus Christ, we have what the world needs: timeless, unchanging, dependable, and knowable truth. Our world is in desperate need of a Savior, and we have the opportunity, the obligation, to tell others. First and foremost, we need to be teaching this truth to our kids. From the time they are born, we need to be singing into their little ears.

"Jesus loves me, this I know, for the Bible tells me so."

"The B-I-B-L-E, yes, that's the Book for me!"

"My God is so big, so strong and so mighty. There's nothing my God cannot do for you!"

These songs should become classics in our homes. From there we can and should advance our children to "Holy, Holy, Holy," "Great Is Thy Faithfulness," and "How Firm a Foundation."

The apostle Paul wrote that mankind has chosen to suppress the truth and has subsequently been overtaken by darkness. Yet he said that "man is without excuse" when it comes to the overwhelming evidence of God's existence and creation (Romans 1:20). This passage reminds us that the world doesn't want God. People know intuitively that this would mean He has authority in their lives and deserve their worship. They've exchanged the truth for a lie—the lie that says there is no God. But if we teach our young children that all of creation points to a

Creator, then they will already be on the path to truth.

We need to begin discussing with them the wonders of God as seen in the handiwork of his creation. These discussions cannot start too early. When my kids were still infants, I would hold them up to the window and say, "Look at the beautiful day God has given us to enjoy!" Throughout our day I would look for evidences of God's creativity—spider webs, caterpillars, rays of sunshine, rainbows, lightning, flowers, leaves—anything to point them to the one true God.

I long for my children to be in awe of the God of wonder. I want them to look for signs of His handiwork:

> *"But ask the animals, and they will teach you,*
> *or the birds of the air, and they will tell you;*
> *or speak to the earth, and it will teach you,*
> *or let the fish of the sea inform you.*
> *Which of all these does not know*
> *that the hand of the Lord has done this?*
> *In his hand is the life of every creature*
> *and the breath of all mankind."*
> (Job 12:7–10)

I want my kids to be intrigued by Him, to be wowed by Him. I want my children to know Him and to love Him. I want them to seek Him, to find Him, and to embrace Him. I pray that they will desire His truth in their lives more than anything else the world can offer them.

Six Facts About Truth

Today's culture embraces the idea of "relative truth." This is the idea that truth changes from person to person, moment to moment, day to day, and situation to situation. But God's Word teaches us that there is a truth that is foundational, a truth we can depend on and build our lives on. Allow me to share with you six facts about truth that I think can be helpful in this discussion.

The first truth about truth is that it exists. In other words, there *are* answers to life's questions—real truth that we are to live by.

Second, these truths are knowable. Truth is something that the average person can understand.

Third, truth is objective, not subjective. This means that truth is the truth regardless of how we feel about it.

Fourth, truth is universal, not cultural. This means

what is true in America is true in Africa, in Europe, in China, anywhere and everywhere. Truth transcends customs and traditions.

Fifth, truth is absolute, which means that truth is always true. Truth doesn't change with the passage of time. What was true for Abraham, Moses, Gideon, Ruth, Solomon, Nehemiah, Esther, John the Baptist, Peter, and Paul is true today and will be true for my children, their children, and their children's children.

Sixth, truth is exclusive. Another way to say this is to say that truth, the answers to life's questions, exclude their opposites.

It might be easier to explain using a simple math equation: 2 + 2 = 4.

1. Truth exists. This means there's an answer to the problem of 2 + 2. We don't have to wonder if there is an answer. There is.

2. Truth is knowable. Not only is there an answer to the equation, the answer is understandable. Using manipulatives, we can "see" the answer and grasp the meaning.

3. Truth is objective. 2 + 2 = 4, no matter how I feel about it. I may not want it to equal 4 because of some negative consequence that an answer of 4 might mean to me personally, but that does not change the answer. The answer is not dependent on how I feel about it.

4. Truth is universal. The answer to the problem of 2 + 2 is the same around the world, from the most sophisticated cities to the most primitive of villages.

5. Truth is absolute. 2 + 2 was equal to 4 when Noah was watching over the animals in the ark, when Joshua was marching around Jericho, when Joseph and Mary participated in the census, and when Jesus rose from the tomb. 2 + 2 = 4 has been true throughout time. It is factual and has not changed.

6. Truth is exclusive. The 2 + 2 = 4 equation has only one answer. There are not multiple possible answers. 2 + 2 does not equal 3 or 5 or 4.13 or −12. 2 + 2 = 4, period.

Now, let's apply these six facts to the gospel.

Truth exists, God exists, and truth is embodied in the person of Jesus (John 1:1–14; Hebrews 1:1–3). Truth is knowable through an ongoing growing relationship with Jesus and through study of God's Word (John 8:31–32; John 17:17). God's truth is objective and is not subject to my whims, wishes, or emotions (Psalm 96:13; Romans 1:19–22). The truth found in God's Word is universal and appropriate for the entire world (Acts 17:26–27). God's truth has always been true. It has not changed, and it will not change (Matthew 24:35; Hebrews 13:8). Finally, truth is exclusive. The ultimate answer to life's questions is found in the person of Jesus Christ and no other (John 14:6).

Freedom!

God's Word says that we will know the truth and the truth will set us free (John 8:32). What is this truth that will set us free? Jesus. He is the way, the truth, and the life (John 14:6). The truth speaks to our sinful condition and offers the only solution—the blood sacrifice of a perfect Lamb. This is a price we could never pay. No matter how much worldly wealth we amass, we cannot buy a righteousness acceptable to a perfect and holy God. The good news is that Jesus freely paid the price. If we will simply believe, call on the name of Jesus, and accept His gift of salvation, we will have new life.

So the truth will set us free, but set us free from what? Christ's truth breaks the lies of the enemy, the chains of sin, and the eternal penalty of death (a.k.a. separation from God). His life, sacrifice, and resurrection have made freedom available to all who will receive it. There's no small print, no "catch." The offer is available to everyone everywhere, anytime in any place, no matter what (Romans 3:22).

We all are born sinful and are doomed to die (Romans 5:12), so why doesn't everyone take God up on His offer of eternal life? It usually comes down to an issue of authority. Some people—most, actually—do not like the idea of having to answer to an Almighty God, of not being able to do whatever they want whenever they want. And they certainly don't like the idea that they can never be good enough. Of course, not liking it doesn't make it any less true. But it leaves us open to the deception of the enemy and the consequences of rejecting the Son of God.

The earlier we can begin discussing the truth with our kids, the more firmly rooted it will become in their hearts and minds. By the world's standards it may sound heartless, but we need to make our children aware of their sinful nature and their need for a Savior.

Life-Giving Truth

Moses admonishes over and over to remember, don't forget, teach your kids. He tells us to impress God's commands upon our children as we sit at home, when we walk or drive along the road, when we lie down, and when we get up (Deuteronomy 6:7).

Teaching our children the truth will help to eliminate rudeness from your home. Love "is not rude" (1 Corinthians 13:5).

Teaching truth takes care of laziness. "Whatever you do, work at it with all your heart, as working for the Lord" (Colossians 3:23).

Teaching truth trains children in obedience. "Children, obey your parents in everything, for this pleases the Lord" (Colossians 3:20).

Teaching truth takes care of sharing. "Share with God's people who are in need" (Romans 12:13).

Teaching truth takes care of discipline. God "disciplines those he loves" (Hebrews 12:6).

Teaching truth takes care of impatience, lying, stealing, lust, and cheating.

Teaching truth takes care of everything.

The truth of Christ as revealed in God's Word holds the answers to all of life's questions, temptations. and trials. As Moses said to the people, "These words are not just idle words for you—they are your life" (Deuteronomy 32:47).

Jesus is the resurrection and the life (John 11:25), the living water (John 7:38), and the light of the world (John 9:5). "His divine power has given us everything we need for life and godliness through our knowledge of him who called us by his own glory and goodness" (2 Peter 1:3). Did you get that? Everything we need is summed up in our knowledge of Him. Moses said, "I have set before you life and death, blessings and curses. Now choose life." Choose Jesus. Choose truth. And by all means teach it to your children "so that you and your children may live" (Deuteronomy 30:19).

A Firm Foundation

We need to regularly open the Word of Life and read it to our children. In the words of the classic hymn, "How firm a foundation, ye saints of the Lord, is laid for your faith in His excellent Word!" Contained in His words are the promises, prophecies, and people God raised up to enact His plans for our benefit and encouragement. We are so blessed to have the Bible, but many of us take it for granted and rarely read from its pages.

There are two important indications of the value we place on God's Word: the personal time we spend in it and the time we spend reading it with our children. As a homeschooling mom, I wouldn't think of neglecting math, science, history, or literature. Most people would agree that to leave any of these subjects out of our curriculum would mean short-changing our kids by compromising their academic experience. But what about their spiritual development, which is far more important? Of all the books we need to read aloud to our kids—and teach them to read themselves—the Bible must be our top priority. There is no excuse for us to neglect this responsibility. We need to take every opportunity to teach our children about God, His Son, and our Helper.

As we read God's Word to our kids, we must point out His many promises of provision, help, comfort, defense, hope, strength, peace, salvation, deliverance, and forgiveness. We must talk of the many Old Testament prophecies concerning the coming of Christ, all of which have been fulfilled, as well as the as-yet-unfulfilled prophecies related to the time when Jesus will return to claim His own.

We must also speak to our children of God's promises made to ordinary people and how their lives were changed in extraordinary ways. Some chose God, and some chose themselves. Some chose to obey, while others chose to run away or rebel. Yet God was always faithful. He did what He said He would do. Our kids need to know that He is the consummate Promise Keeper.

Heroes of the Faith

In addition to teaching our children the Word, we would do well to share with them other real-life examples of the faith. Our kids need to see that God still moves, still keeps His promises, still calls people, and still strengthens, defends, provides, equips, protects, and intercedes.

We have made it a regular part of our home school to read biographies of great men and women of God. Together we revel in the adventures of missionaries and others who sought God's will for their lives and set out on grand adventures for His glory. George Müller, Mary Slessor, David Livingston, Sundar Singh, Charles Wesley—these were men and women who lived like they were dying, venturing forth with reckless abandon for the sake of the gospel. We have traveled the world with these bold believers as they faced witch doctors and black magic, went before kings and chiefs, battled lions and depression, and birthed and buried children. In our readings, we have traveled by boat, plane, train, caravan, canoe, donkey, camel, car, and sedan chair. (Read the biography of Lottie Moon to find out about sedan chairs.) We have been heartbroken over their losses, excited by their successes, and saddened by their deaths.

As we have read these heroes' stories, our family has dared to imagine what God might call *us* to. When times got tough and challenges came our way, we drew strength from their examples of faith, trust, and dependence on God.

We have also sought to develop relationships with present-day missionaries, cultivating friendships with men and women serving in locations across the globe. I was blessed to have parents who had a heart for missions, and I have fond memories of having visiting missionaries to our home for dinner and listening to their stories of life in the mission field.

We must put godly examples of faithful living in our children's path. We are raising the next generation of world changers, and need to have people in their lives who reinforce what we are teaching. Ask for God's provision in this area, then wait and see whom He sends to bless your kids and inspire them to do great things for Him.

Living Out Loud

Of course, you can read the Bible and missionary biographies daily to your kids, but if you don't live out loud what you are reading out loud, the time spent will be fruitless. The effect of such hypocrisy can be devastating in the lives of your children.

In teaching truth, it is important that you live a life according to the truth. Live as someone who loves truth, pursues truth, values truth, and prioritizes truth. Live as someone who regularly sacrifices, encourages, and promotes truth in order to pass it on, teach it, and instill it. You must live truth every day and in front of your kids. It's not enough to breathe life into hundred- and thousand-year-old stories, no matter how factual and inspiring. Your personal and daily example will either negate or reinforce what you read.

As parents, we can easily become content to maintain the status quo, uninterested in further sacrifice, discipline, growth, or challenge in our own lives. Sure, our kids need to mature; we see that clearly enough. But what about ourselves? Too often, we're willing to settle for good enough or far enough or just enough. Yet God loves us too much to leave us in the comfortable place of "enough." He pursues our total transformation so that one day the Father can say, "Well done, good and faithful servant!"

Somewhere, as a young woman, I had adopted the

notion that we all grow up and mature to a certain point—somewhere in our thirties or forties—and then we coast the rest of the way until death or the rapture arrives. I thought adults just kind of arrived at a certain level of insight or wisdom after having made the necessary sacrifices along the way. Then they got to set the auto-pilot and coast in. Somehow I had come to think there was a vague, far-off point where all of life's dues had been paid and a person could just rest on his or her laurels and encourage others toward the great beyond.

Boy was I wrong. There's no coasting this side of heaven.

The process of sanctification takes no vacations. It doesn't account for the economy, the holidays, tragedies, the weather, celebrations, or anything else. In God's economy nothing is wasted. Every failure, every victory, every life, every death, every gain, every loss—He works all things together for the sanctification and ultimate good of those who love Him (Romans 8:28). All things. Laundry, grocery shopping, math lessons, sibling rivalry, cross-country moves, employment, unemployment, friendships, churches, all things.

Meanwhile, we are to live a life worthy of that to which we have been called. We live truth when we do the laundry with a grateful and joyful heart. We live truth at the grocery store when we greet the workers, shop responsibly, and give a smile to our fellow customers. We live truth as we teach our kids math by exhibiting patience, perseverance, gentleness, and hope. When we address conflicts between our children we have an opportunity to exemplify grace and mercy. If we lose our jobs, we can stand firm on His faithfulness, live without worry, and look to Him to be our provider in all things.

We can live truth by allowing it to set us free from worry, panic, exhaustion, and despair. Trust me, you will stand out from the crowd when you reject the "normal" worldly responses to the stress of everyday living. In doing so, we are often given opportunities to shine like stars, to testify to His goodness and grace, His provision and protection, and His love for His own.

When we live boldly, by faith and in truth, we join the mothers and fathers who pass the baton to their children by putting their own faith into action. I remember watching my parents work through some tough situations. Many times I saw my dad take a courageous stand, with my mom at his side. Similarly, my kids need to see my faith, not just hear about it.

Live out loud whatever God has called you to do for His glory. We must not fall into the trap of thinking that because we live average, seemingly mundane lives our examples don't matter. When we strive to live like we belong to God, our children will gain far more from watching us than from reading any biography. Our lives are books—living books—the pages of which we fill every day. We must write on these "pages" wisely, intentionally, and carefully. Ours may not be lives worthy of a published account, they may not be especially exciting or adventurous, but if they are lived in absolute obedience to the King of kings and Lord of lords, then they will speak volumes.

Hiding His Word

There are many who wrongly believe that children cannot memorize more than a few words of Scripture. They are selling kids short. Children come pre-wired to memorize God's Word. Psalm 8:2 says that "from the lips of children and infants you have ordained praise."

I have seen this in the lives of my own children. Having never been challenged as a child to memorize scripture regularly, we were shocked to see what enrollment in a nearby AWANA program did to revolutionize our family goals in terms of scripture memory. Davis and I couldn't believe what the books were challenging our kids to do. And they rose to the challenge, putting most adults to shame in this particular spiritual discipline. Davis became involved as an AWANA leader and eventually rose to the highest rank as commander of an entire club.

I was convicted as I realized I had fallen prey to yet another of the enemy's lies—the one that said I was incapable of memorizing scriptures. After all, I could still sing the lyrics to songs I hadn't heard in decades (many of which I was ashamed I knew). Oh, I could memorize. I had simply not taken the time to focus my mind on the truth of God's Word and hide it in my heart.

We began using the AWANA curriculum as an integral part of our daily routine. We practiced the verses every morning before, during, and after breakfast. A few years ago, AWANA initiated an annual event challenging participants to memorize longer passages, usually thirteen verses in length. We tackled these as a family. Together we memorized Isaiah 53, 1 Corinthians 13, Ephesians 2, Ephesians 6, Philippians 4, Proverbs 3, John 10, and many others. After our club discontinued the program, Davis chose passages for us, and we continued the practice as part of our dinner table conversation. I was constantly amazed at how even the youngest of our kids memorized the passages, often with more ease than Davis or myself.

It remains a continuing habit for us to be memorizing a passage together. Recently we took on our biggest goal ever—the entire book of Jonah. You should see six-year-old Benjamin quote the portion we have completed so far. Even with some minor mispronunciations, it is powerful.

Hiding the Word intentionally in the hearts of our children is the most fundamental foundation we can lay in their hearts. It's like the sealant we put on their teeth that guards against decay. It's like the vitamins we give them to fortify their systems. It's like the well-balanced meals we provide to help them grow physically strong. It's like the habits of making their bed, saying "please" and "thank you," and looking both ways before crossing the street. Like these habits, hiding the Word in their hearts will keep them safe while building their character and self-discipline (Psalm 119:11).

In the End, They Must Choose

Could it be described as spiritual neglect if we do not teach our children to meditate upon and memorize God's Word, His truth? Indeed, it would be the highest form of neglect. Let it not be so of us.

And yet we must know that just as God gave you and me free will, our kids also have free will. One of my children asked me, "What is the hardest part of being a parent?" I replied, "It is the sobering knowledge that each of you is a free agent and that you have a relentless enemy. I love you all so much. I can pray for you and I always will, but I cannot *choose* for you. The good news is that understanding this keeps me praying, and I know that He who is in you is greater than he who is in the world" (1 John 4:4).

Isaac, Solomon, Samuel, Daniel, Timothy—all of these young men had been taught and trained well. According to Hebrew tradition, they would have memorized the entire Torah by the age of ten. Not *passages* of the Torah—the *whole* Torah. Do you suppose that affected their hearts? Do you think their knowledge may have affected their actions? Samuel and Daniel are especially amazing examples of young men who rose to the occasions providentially presented to them. They chose well when it was their moment, and they stood tall in faith.

The Bible also gives some startling examples of children who ought to have known better, given the biblical accounts we have of their parents. Cain, Esau, Ishmael, Samson, Absalom—what went wrong with them? Their parents seemed like great people. So what happened?

Each of them was given a choice. Samson is arguably the best biblical example of a young man who chose poorly. Scripture makes it clear that his parents desired to be good parents. They inquired of God to "teach" them how to raise him (Judges 13:8). Throughout the next few chapters of Judges, it is abundantly clear that Samson knew better and had been taught better than his actions might lead an outside observer to believe. Samson had opportunity after opportunity to make good choices, but over and over again he made selfish, foolish choices. The account is heartbreaking to read.

As parents we must accept the responsibility to teach our children diligently, but we cannot choose for them. We can pray for them, but we cannot live their lives. We can advise them, but we cannot force them to accept God's will. We must be willing to let go, knowing that He loves our children more than we do.

Sing the Wondrous Love of Jesus

I am grateful for many aspects of my upbringing. I am blessed with a Christian heritage that goes back several generations. One family heritage I am especially thankful for is the old hymns. Being raised as preacher's kids, we always sat in the front row. Both my parents would sing out strong and harmonize, and I treasured the sound.

I still keep an old hymnal that I usually reference in my laundry room as I fold clothes, or in the kitchen as I cook. The words from these songs soothe me like nothing else. I have stood with hands held high in praise and joy, and I have knelt with cheeks washed in tears as I have been barely able to hum.

What a friend we have in Jesus,
all our sins and grief to bear!
What a privilege to carry
everything to Him in prayer!
Immortal, invisible, God only wise,
In light inaccessible hid from our eyes,
Most blessed, most glorious, the Ancient of Days,
Almighty, victorious, Thy great Name we praise.
What can wash away my sin?
Nothing but the blood of Jesus.
What can make me whole again?
Nothing but the blood of Jesus.
On Christ, the solid Rock, I stand.
All other ground is sinking sand.
Sweet hour of prayer!
Sweet hour of prayer!
That calls me from a world of care,
and bids me at my Father's throne
make all my wants and wishes known.
Great is Thy faithfulness,
O God my father!
There is no shadow of turning with Thee.

Thou changest not,
Thy compassions, they fail not;
as thou hast been, Thou forever will be.

What else can I say? We were made to worship.
Songs, and their words, find their way deep into the
conscience, so we must choose them carefully. In Acts
16:25, Paul and Silas were imprisoned with double shack-
les. They had every reason to be miserable, but chose to
sing and pray. Wow! Now there's an example for all of
us: When life is bleakest, when the night is darkest, we
should praise Him!

I had a mentor many years ago who encouraged me
to sing the hymns while I was doing the most mundane
of tasks, those I really didn't enjoy, thereby turning that
chore into a time of worship. This is an example I have
tried to pass on to my children. Worshiping God Almighty is always timely, always appropriate, always helpful, always time well spent.

Singing the great hymns, with their deep and mean-
ingful lyrics, can help teach doctrine while ministering
to the soul. If your kids are at all musically inclined, they

can learn to play the simple melodies, enabling you to share them in communal worship.

The Value of a Family Worship Time

Teaching kids truth is teaching them discernment. We're giving them the primary tool they need to navigate life in this fallen world. Our relativistic culture promotes "truths" that are fluid, individual, relative, and changing. The idea that truth is exclusive to one God, that His truth is definable and unchanging is often considered bigoted and judgmental. Undesirable accusations dog anyone who proposes knowing God's truth or encouraging others to pursue it.

So it is that teaching truth must be done deliberately and daily with determination, focus, and purpose. It must be done with a long-term vision for what God will do over time. We must guide our kids through each teachable moment and demonstrate how to take every thought captive and make it obedient to the truth of God's Word (2 Corinthians 10:5).

There are many ways to do this, but the one I think is most important is to set the tone for the day by hav-

ing morning worship as a family. Setting a regular time
to read Scripture and pray and sing praises sets the stage
for teaching truth. No competent movie director would
set a western on the moon, or a Civil War epic in the
Caribbean, or an underwater odyssey in the Sahara. The
context and setting matter. Props, costumes, incidental
action—they all matter. A good movie fits together like
a jigsaw puzzle: Nothing is out of place and everything
has a purpose. Everything ultimately points back to the
theme and reinforces the main point.

Our homes should be like that. They should be well-
thought-out, purposeful places of learning and worship
that constantly, consistently, and completely point our
kids to the truth of God, His Word, and His plan for
their lives. Regular family worship sets the stage for their
day. It puts first things first and sets a tone of praise, submission, service, and sacrifice. Old Testament law taught
the value of "firstfruits" (Exodus 23:19), and in the New
Testament Jesus admonished His followers to "seek first
the kingdom of God" (Matthew 6:33, ESV). When we set
aside the first part of our morning for worship of Him,
He blesses us. He knows what our day will hold even

before we rise, and it is His desire to prepare us for it, individually and as a family.

Believe me, this next generation *wants* to make a difference. They want to live lives that matter. They want to do something significant, difficult, bold, and world-changing. Setting the stage for their days and for their lives will encourage our kids to become all that God has planned them to be.

As you go before the throne of grace with confidence as a family, God will pour out His wisdom, love, grace, and truth. So praise His name!

HEART CHECKUP

1. Are you currently building the foundation of your home on the rock-solid truth of Jesus Christ and the Bible?

2. In 1 Peter 3:15, we are told to be prepared to give an answer. How are you preparing yourself and your children to give answers?

3. From what inferior sources are your children picking up their information? How are you teaching them to stand firm in the truth that you have taught them?

4. In Deuteronomy 6:7, we are charged to teach our children diligently. What are some of the ways you can begin to do this today?

Epilogue
Heartfelt Encouragement

Therefore, since we are surrounded by such a great cloud of witnesses, let us throw off everything that hinders and the sin that so easily entangles, and let us run with perseverance the race marked out for us. Let us fix our eyes on Jesus, the author and perfecter of our faith, who for the joy set before him endured the cross, scorning its shame, and sat down at the right hand of the throne of God. Consider him who endured such opposition from sinful men, so that you will not grow weary and lose heart.

Hebrews 12:1–3

Hebrews 11 is one of my favorite scriptures, as it recounts the Heroes of the Faith. It's not an exhaustive list, but it does mention many who stood firm against the raging storms of life, in the dark times, or at times of great opposition. This passage has been a source of inspiration as I considered my own Christian heritage and the baton I hope to pass on to my children.

Then comes Hebrews 12.

"Therefore," it begins. In other words, "in light of the fact that these others have gone before, this is what you should do." What follows is an admonishment to those of us who desire to follow in their footsteps of heroes, who long to pick up where they left off, who long to be counted among the faithful.

Throw Off Entanglements

The author of Hebrews writes, "Let us throw off everything that hinders and the sin that so easily entangles" (Hebrews 12:1). An entanglement is anything that is keeping you from pursuing God, or specific to our topic, anything that is keeping you from having a heart for your kids. So what is holding you back? What makes you hesitate? What gives you pause?

Some of my own entanglements have included my expectations, my agendas, my selfish ambitions, my wrong thinking, and my messed-up priorities. In short, I was the one getting in the way of developing a heart for my kids. I was under the mistaken impression that having kids was all about me, that they were supposed to make me look good and feel good. I expected them to be cooperative, compliant, and cute.

But God knew better. I needed to have a whole heart for Him so I would be able to give my heart to my kids. Only then would they desire to give their hearts to Him. God knew my heart was puffed up, that I had to die to myself, and as I did, my entanglements would lessen and my race would become easier to run.

In Hebrews 12, the command is given for us to throw off our entanglements. Isn't that interesting? We are supposed to not only be aware of those things that hinder and entangle us, but we must also choose to dispose of them so that we can run our race better. We are supposed to see our entanglements like God sees them—as inhibitive, as burdens, as cumbersome and unnecessary weights He wants us to lay aside.

What is holding you back from running well the race set before you? What are the entanglements that are keeping you from having a healthy heart?

Run with Perseverance

The Hebrews writer goes on to say, "Let us run with perseverance the race marked out for us" (Hebrews 12:1). I love this picture: God calls us to run, not walk. I guess there will be plenty of time for casual strolling when we arrive home, and I am looking forward to that. But He advises us to run here on earth. Running implies a certain level of commitment as well as a good bit of training. Runners also must have a goal in mind—a finish line.

Running is a discipline; it is not for the lazy person. It takes time to prepare for a race, and there are many decisions to be made along the way. Runners invest a good deal of time and money training for the big race. They do not just lace up their sneakers and run. In order to do well, they must demand more of themselves, deny themselves, and push themselves.

You need to be determined to run the race that God has marked out specifically for you. You are not called to run someone else's race. The race that is set before you is different from the one He set before me. We are unique and so are our journeys through this life. Run the course

God marked out for you. The Master of the universe has personally laid out your course, providentially taking into account your strengths and weaknesses. He has chosen your path and has promised to provide His light to guide you.

In Hebrews, we are told not just to run, but to run with perseverance. That means determination. That means endurance. We are to set our faces as flint and run with purpose, knowing we will not be put to shame (Isaiah 50:7). We are not to dilly-dally but to set our pace and go. We are to run, knowing that it is not a short race but, rather, a marathon complete with seasons of struggle and storms as well as seasons of rebirth and renewal.

Perseverance means that we don't give up, we don't sit down, and we don't turn back. Perseverance means that we stay on course despite the doubts, the conflicts, the criticism, the attacks, and the trials, all the way to the finish. Running with perseverance means that we don't give up on Him, remembering that He who is in us is greater than he who is in the world (1 John 4:4). We need to take our Lord at His word. He who began a good work in you will see it through to completion (Philippians 1:6).

Believe that He is able to do exceedingly, abundantly more than you could ever ask or imagine (Ephesians 3:20)!

Fix Your Eyes on Jesus

When I was a little girl I would playfully cross my eyes, and Mom would tell me if I didn't stop they would get stuck that way. As a mother myself, I have become convinced that we all need to become "Cross-eyed." We need to "fix our eyes on Jesus" who endured the cross for us (Hebrews 12:2).

If our eyes are fixed on Christ and His redemptive work on the cross, this will make all the difference. If we choose to view the world around us, the people we interact with, and the problems we are facing through Cross-eyes, it will change everything. We will see the world differently if we look at it through the lens of Christ's sacrifice and His love poured out on Calvary. We will see our neighbors, our friends, our family, our mailman, the grocery clerk, and the hotel attendant differently if we see them as Jesus sees them. Jesus has already paid their debt, if they would but receive Him and accept it.

Fixing our eyes, though, is not easily done. Our enemy is a master at distraction and deception. He is brilliant at flashing lights and bling in our faces to draw us away from the truth. Our eyes begin to wander and stray from Jesus toward things, stuff, and self. Jesus and the cross can be difficult to look upon, so we choose an image that's more appetizing or easier on the eyes. In a trance-like state we give our allegiance over to another. Wild-eyed, we run after empty promises, down dead-end roads at top speed. We reach the end and wonder how we got there. We forget where we were going, then realize we have lost our way.

Like the patient father of the prodigal child, our heavenly Father welcomes us back as we fix our eyes back on His Son and make our way back to the Light. We can see clearly now, and we are so grateful to be back on the right path.

Focus is something we must fight for. It is not easily maintained. You must daily fix your eyes on Jesus, daily choosing to abide in Him, daily choosing to walk in the Light, and daily choosing to seek God with all your heart.

Consider Christ

I remember when Davis and I went to see *The Passion of the Christ* during its initial release. While I was getting dressed to go, I remember thinking how strange it felt to be getting dressed up to go to a crucifixion. Hairspray and lip balm seemed unimportant. When we arrived to the theater, there were people standing in line to buy popcorn and a Coke. Really? I'm not writing to endorse the movie or advocate that you see it, except to say that it is a powerful portrayal of Christ's sacrifice. The imagery was intense. I suppose you could be in the audience and tune it out, but there was a teenage boy beside me who was reduced to sobs. Jesus' pain and suffering were so vivid on screen and yet somehow so personal. It was an overwhelming experience.

While the cross is arguably the twist in the story, the point where everything seems to have gone wrong for Satan—the blow from which there can be no recovery—is the resurrection. That is the real climax. Sunday morning is when the irony became clear. Hope was born, joy was declared, and love was celebrated.

Consider the cross. As we keep our eyes on Jesus, we gain strength. When we study this Man who had compassion on the masses, healed individuals, spoke to the storm, and raised the dead, we gain a new perspective on those around us, the task before us, and the opportunities we are facing. In Hebrews 12:3, we are instructed to "consider Him who endured such opposition from sinful men so that we do not grow weary or lose heart." The implication seems to be that by keeping our focus on Christ and contemplating His sacrifice, we are defending ourselves—a kind of protection against growing weary and losing heart.

When we consider Him as our example, we are inspired by His endurance to the opposition. His opposition was so extreme that they nailed Him to a cross. I suspect that you have faced opposition sometime in your life. I know I have. It's hard when people do and say tacky or thoughtless things. I have known the pain of betrayal, lies, vindictiveness, jealously, and spite. Many times I have been reduced to tears, and even today I have tender scars where someone hurt me. But then, I haven't been nailed to a tree, I haven't been stoned, and I haven't been fed to hungry lions. Christ faced His opposition head-on, and He endured it. Isaiah 53:7 says, "He was oppressed and afflicted, yet he did not open his mouth." He endured.

When we come up against opposition, and we certainly will if we live a life worthy—if we dare to dream, if we love our spouses, if we raise our kids to love Him, if we live lives of reckless abandon, and yes, if we home educate—then we must endure. We must consider Christ, set our jaws, and walk confidently forward in our calling. There will be times we are tempted to waver, moments when we want to sit down or give up, and it is in those moments that we must hold tight to the image of our Lord as they nailed Him to the cross. This was when His resolve to submit to the Father's will was symbolized by His laying down His life for us.

Do Not Grow Weary or Lose Heart

In Galatians 6:9 (NASB), Paul writes, "Let us not lose heart in doing good, for in due time we will reap if we do not grow weary." This is one of those commands in Scripture that doesn't get much attention, but is a key point in our maintaining the course. Do you ever tire of being patient, being nice, being forgiving, being gracious, or being long-suffering? Am I the only one who would like to be done with the mundane tasks of toilet cleaning, laundry, dusting, sweeping, cooking, shopping, vacuuming or scrubbing? Surely not.

Let's look at this command a little closer. First of all, this is not a suggestion. Paul doesn't say, "try not to." He says imperatively, "Let us not." We are told not to lose heart. This would suggest that we had our hearts to start with. This implies that our hearts were doing what they were supposed to be doing and focusing on what they were supposed to focus on. You cannot lose something you don't have. In this case, we're talking about your heart.

We are also told to "not grow weary." So what are some of the things we need to do and not grow weary? Well, we should not grow weary expressing and practicing the fruit of the Spirit: love, joy, peace, patience, kindness, goodness, faithfulness, gentleness, and self-control. In addition, we should guard against growing weary in service of our families. This can include doing the laundry, preparing the meals, cleaning toilets, cleaning house, and encouraging our husbands. How about staying the course, humbling ourselves, or choosing joy? These are just some of the things this scripture is charging us to pursue. We are to keep on keeping on even when it's hard, even after we have done it a million times, and even when we plain don't want to.

I am getting ready to plant our garden for the year. Our plans include planting tomatoes, peppers, green beans, squash, sunflowers, and a few herbs. We have already tilled the soil a couple of times, enriching it with fertilizer from our compost pile. Savannah Anne, Molly, and Elizabeth have planned out the rows and placement. We have some seedlings we've grown ourselves under the light hut, but we will also be purchasing others from a local nursery. After planting, we will water the seedlings and wait for them to grow, bloom, and eventually, produce a harvest. In the meantime, weeds will sprout up and we will have to be attentive to pull the weeds as soon as they are spotted.

There is a particular weed, a vine actually, that we have to catch while it is young because when it matures it grows thorns and is almost impossible to remove. If you aren't diligent about weeding, they will take over the place and choke out the other plants—the ones we actually chose, purchased, and planted. That is what Paul means when he exhorts us to not wait and let the weariness set in.

Now, I am in no way denying how hard this all is. Homeschooling is hard. This parenting thing is downright frustrating at times. Therefore, we must nurture the positive and guard against the negative. Whining, complaining, grumbling, and being difficult, cranky, or grumpy are attitudes we cannot afford to allow to take root in our homes.

You are the one who will choose your mindset. You are the one who chooses your focus. You are the one who chooses your perspective and your responses. You need to make sure you are choosing wisely. You have been given an awesome opportunity to raise your children to live lives of service to the God of the universe. Therefore do not grow weary!

Acknowledgments

This project began over nineteen years ago when I first became a mom. I remember the first time I presented the ideas in this book to an audience at a homeschool conference in North Carolina. Immediately after the workshop, several attendees told me I had to write a book. Writing a book was the last thing on my mind back then, as I was about to celebrate the first birthday of my fifth child.

Yet here it is. So I would like to thank those moms and dads who attended this particular workshop and encouraged me over and over to share these ideas in written form with a larger audience. This book was their idea before it was mine.

Thank you, Zan Tyler. I originally pitched this idea to you when you were with another publishing house. Now we work together side by side. I am grateful that God brought us together. Your experience as a mother, wife, and homeschool advocate has blessed the lives of countless families. As you set out on your own homeschool journey, you could not have known how far-reaching the impact would be. God has used your journey to inspire many to step out in faith and begin their own adventure. And your friendship means the world to me. Every time we are together I wish we had more time, and I leave looking forward to the next time we can get together! I could never thank you adequately for all you have taught me and for the many times you have encouraged me.

Thank you, David Webb. Talk about irony of ironies. I first met David when he too was with another publishing house. I was shopping a couple of book ideas and had the privilege of sitting down to talk with David. In ways that only God could do, He has since brought David to the Apologia team as an author in his own right (the What We Believe series) and also as my editor on this project. David has been beyond patient with me as I fought to actually get him something to edit. The best thing about David is that I trust him completely to maintain my voice and yet improve my clarity and poignancy. David is also one of my favorite people to talk with, as he has had such a wide variety of life experiences. Thank you, David, for working to make my writing the best it can be.

Thank you, Davis. Our life together has been such an amazing journey, though nothing like either of us would have ever dreamed! God has been so good and gracious to us. Thank you for encouraging me to "keep on" when I have been tired and weary. Thank you for reminding me of God's willingness to pour out His grace and mercy. Thank you for all of the dates you take me on, for still chasing me around the house, for the early morning walks, and the late night talks. I love being loved by you. You are my Beloved! Your love for me and the kids is selfless and genuine. I am grateful for how much time and energy you give to our family. Thank you for the hours you put into reading over my chapters. I know that your priority is to help me say what I am meaning to say. Thank you for helping me with my wordiness but respecting my unique style. I love you!

Thanks to my kids: Charles, Anderson, Savannah Anne, Molly, Elizabeth, Joseph, and Benjamin. I am grateful for each of you. God has taught me so much during our days together. Thank you for your words of encouragement, for all of the hugs, and for honoring my time when I needed to write. Thanks for celebrating with me the night I finished.

Charles, being the oldest is a role chosen for only a few. You have lived up to the position by inspiring your siblings and challenging them to work hard.

Anderson, God picked you to be the perfect sidekick for your older brother. I know that has included many a rough-and-tumble, but you have fit well your role as second oldest, a sea of calm amid the storm. You are my own personal encourager.

Charles and Anderson, my own immaturity made life more difficult for you in the early days as I was learning. This whole book really started with you two. You two made me smile and laugh as I watched your relationship as brothers grow. You both challenged the way I thought about God and myself. You two made me want to be a better mom; you made me want to sacrifice myself; you made me want to go deeper in my relationship with God. The two of you introduced me to frogs, anoles, and caterpillars. And the two of you shared the joys of our growing family. Thank you.

Savannah Anne, your smile is beautiful and your personal pursuit of God along with your diligence is an inspiration. I am grateful for the softening you brought to our family from the very beginning.

Molly, your passion and strength are incredible. Your bright eyes light up our home. Your desire to pursue God is an honor to Him.

Elizabeth, you have the gentle and quiet spirit extolled in Scripture. You have also been gifted with a servant's heart. Your attitude is such a blessing.

Joseph and Benjamin, I am so grateful that the two of you have each other. In many ways it is like watching Charles and Anderson all over again. The two of you do everything with all of your energy, whether you're playing with LEGO bricks, kicking a soccer ball, riding your bikes, or playing at the pool. I enjoy our discussions about God, His creation, and heaven most of all. Your questions make me smile.

God has big plans for all of you, my children, and I am honored to have a front-row seat!

Finally, I want to thank all the friends who have walked with me through this process. Laura Silver and Carolyn Atkinson are my early Wednesday morning friends. Your prayers, laughter, and encouraging words have carried me through many a discouragement. Thank you for holding my arms up, for loving me, and for extending me grace. I love you.

Thank you also to Lorie Kirkland. During this period we both graduated our oldest sons and watched as they took flight. God has been so gracious to show us His provision in countless ways. I look forward to many other times together rejoicing in His goodness. Your friendship is a blessing, and you are a beautiful reflection of the King.

Thank you to the entire Apologia Family. Thanks especially to Liz Corson, who is simply a joy to know. Her personal strength and dependability are a blessing. Her love for her family is beautiful and selfless. Thank you also to Charity Lesh, who has been my personal assistant. Charity, you helped me in thousands of ways and took a big load off my mind. Thank you for chasing ideas and dreams of mine so that I could focus on my kids and my man. I am looking forward to working with all of you for many years to come. And what's better, I am looking forward to sharing eternity with you all!

Last, but not least, thank you to Lisa Nance, Becky Justice, and all the moms involved in the HELP (Home Educators at Lee Park) co-op during 2009–2010. Leading and participating in my first co-op in the same year was not the best idea I've ever conceived, but God was faithful. Thank you all for your kindnesses and patience as we worked through it all. Watching each of you navigate your homeschool journey this last year has taught me again about the importance of depending on and trusting God. He is always faithful. May He abundantly bless each of you and your families!